The Censorship Debate

Editor: Tracy Biram

Volume 347

Independence Educational Publishers

First published by Independence Educational Publishers

The Studio, High Green

Great Shelford

Cambridge CB22 5EG

England

© Independence 2019

Copyright

Photocopy licence

ISBN-13: 978 1 86168 803 3

Printed in Great Britain

Zenith Print Group

Contents

Introduction

THE CENSORSHIP DEBATE is Volume 347 in the **ISSUES** series. The aim of the series is to offer current, diverse information about important issues in our world, from a UK perspective.

ABOUT THE CENSORSHIP DEBATE

All of us are affected by censorship every day, from what we watch on the TV, to what we read in the news. But just how much are we actually affected? The UK is now one of the worst places in Europe for press freedom, due to restrictions placed on journalists. Freedom of expression is a fundamental part of our society, but this is not the case in all countries. This book discusses censorship and its forms around the world.

OUR SOURCES

Titles in the **ISSUES** series are designed to function as educational resource books, providing a balanced overview of a specific subject.

The information in our books is comprised of facts, articles and opinions from many different sources, including:

⇨ Newspaper reports and opinion pieces

⇨ Website factsheets

⇨ Magazine and journal articles

⇨ Statistics and surveys

⇨ Government reports

⇨ Literature from special interest groups.

A NOTE ON CRITICAL EVALUATION

Because the information reprinted here is from a number of different sources, readers should bear in mind the origin of the text and whether the source is likely to have a particular bias when presenting information (or when conducting their research). It is hoped that, as you read about the many aspects of the issues explored in this book, you will critically evaluate the information presented.

It is important that you decide whether you are being presented with facts or opinions. Does the writer give a biased or unbiased report? If an opinion is being expressed, do you agree with the writer? Is there potential bias to the 'facts' or statistics behind an article?

ASSIGNMENTS

In the back of this book, you will find a selection of assignments designed to help you engage with the articles you have been reading and to explore your own opinions. Some tasks will take longer than others and there is a mixture of design, writing and research-based activities that you can complete alone or in a group.

Useful weblinks

www.amnesty.org.uk

eandt.theiet.org

www.bbfc.co.uk

www.cam.ac.uk

www.childrenscommissioner.gov.uk

www.diversecymru.org.uk

www.equalityhumanrights.com

www.freemuse.org

www.independent.co.uk

www.inews.co.uk

www.ofcom.org.uk

www.oxplore.org

www.spectator.co.uk

www.spiked-online.com

www.telegraph.co.uk

www.thebureauinvestigates.com

www.theconversation.com

www.theguardian.com

www.whoishostingthis.com

FURTHER RESEARCH

At the end of each article we have listed its source and a website that you can visit if you would like to conduct your own research. Please remember to critically evaluate any sources that you consult and consider whether the information you are viewing is accurate and unbiased.

What is freedom of speech?

Freedom of speech is the right to say whatever you like about whatever you like, whenever you like, right? Wrong.

'Freedom of speech is the right to seek, receive and impart information and ideas of all kinds, by any means.'

Freedom of speech and the right to freedom of expression applies to ideas of all kinds including those that may be deeply offensive. But it comes with responsibilities and we believe it can be legitimately restricted.

When freedom of speech can be restricted

You might not expect us to say this, but in certain circumstances free speech and freedom of expression can be restricted.

Governments have an obligation to prohibit hate speech and incitement. And restrictions can also be justified if they protect specific public interest or the rights and reputations of others.

Any restrictions on freedom of speech and freedom of expression must be set out in laws that must in turn be clear and concise so everyone can understand them.

People imposing the restrictions (whether they are governments, employers or anyone else) must be able to demonstrate the need for them, and they must be proportionate.

All of this has to be backed up by safeguards to stop the abuse of these restrictions and incorporate a proper appeals process.

...and when it can't

Restrictions that do not comply with all these conditions violate freedom of expression.

We consider people put in prison solely for exercising their right to free speech to be prisoners of conscience.

Checks and balances

Specifics

Any restriction should be as specific as possible. It would be wrong to ban an entire website because of a problem with one page.

National security and public order

These terms must be precisely defined in law to prevent them being used as excuses for excessive restrictions.

Morals

This is a very subjective area, but any restrictions must not be based on a single tradition or religion and must not discriminate against anyone living in a particular country.

Rights and reputations of others

Public officials should tolerate more criticism than private individuals. So defamation laws that stop legitimate criticism of a government or public official, violate the right to free speech.

Blasphemy

Protecting abstract concepts, religious beliefs or other beliefs or the sensibilities of people that believe them is not grounds for restricting freedom of speech.

Media and journalists

Journalists and bloggers face particular risks because of the work they do. Countries therefore have a responsibility to protect their right to freedom of speech. Restrictions on newspapers, TV stations, etc. can affect everyone's right to freedom of expression.

Whistleblowers

Government should never bring criminal proceedings against anyone who reveals information about human rights abuses.

Rights and responsibilities

Free speech is one of our most important rights and one of the most misunderstood.

Use your freedom of speech to speak out for those that are denied theirs. But use it responsibly: it is a powerful thing.

Isn't freedom of speech just saying whatever you want?

We too often see unpleasant and untrue things said about marginalised communities, things often verging on incitements to hate or commit acts of hate. The common defence for these statements is 'freedom of speech', which is often interpreted as 'I can say whatever I want and you can't do anything about it'.

While it is important to allow frank exchanges of views and opinions, it is important to understand what is really meant by freedom of speech. In the UK, we are protected by the Human Rights Act, which adheres to Article 10 of the European Convention. There are two parts to this; of which the first guarantees freedom of expression without interference from the state whilst the second says that this freedom is not unrestricted and carries with it 'duties and responsibilities'.

When looking at the first part of Article 10 it is important to note that speech is only protected from interference by the state.

This means that although people can say whatever they want (within the limits of the second part of Article 10), other people are free to both disagree and refuse to provide a venue or method for someone to espouse opinions that they disagree with. This is why, in theory, websites like Twitter or Facebook are allowed to remove or restrict access to opinions they deem offensive and why institutions like universities can refuse to host any speakers or debates they choose to (sometimes known as no-platforming).

This second part of Article 10, which details the restrictions to speech, is also commonly misunderstood or ignored altogether. Reasons speech can be restricted include the following:

⇨ In the interests of national security, territorial integrity or public safety

⇨ For the prevention of disorder or crime

⇨ For the protection of health or morals

⇨ For the protection of the reputation or rights of others

⇨ For preventing the disclosure of information received in confidence

⇨ For maintaining the authority and impartiality of the judiciary.

UK law straddles a tricky line between maintaining freedom of expression whilst banning such things as hate speech. This is difficult as hate speech can sometimes be a subjective issue, but 'threatening, abusive or insulting words or behaviour intending or likely to cause harassment, alarm or distress or cause a breach of the peace' is prohibited.

Unfortunately, there are those who believe such threatening and inciteful behaviour is part of their right to free speech. There are complaints and protests from those who say their rights are being infringed, when in fact it is simply the second part of their right to free speech that is being enforced upon them, which they have chosen to ignore. The two parts cannot be separated. If what someone says is deemed to be hate speech, there are consequences and repercussions.

People can say whatever they want; however, they will be held responsible for those words.

8 February 2016

www.diversecymru.org.uk

The top ten things you need to know about freedom of expression laws

1. Freedom of expression is a fundamental right protected under the Human Rights Act and under British common law.

2. This can extend to the expression of views that may shock, disturb or offend the deeply-held beliefs of others.

3. Any restrictions must always be set out in law and be proportionate.

4. Freedom of expression can be limited and in particular does not protect statements that discriminate against or harass, or incite violence or hatred against, other persons and groups, particularly by reference to their race, religious belief, gender or sexual orientation.

5. No one can rely on the human right to freedom of expression to limit or undermine the human rights of others.

6. It is not always easy to draw the boundary between freely expressing intolerant or offensive views and hate speech. In making the distinction, the speaker's intention, the context, the audience, the particular words used and form of communication will all be taken into account.

7. Freedom of expression is protected more strongly in some contexts than others. In particular, a wide degree of tolerance is accorded to political speech and debate during election campaigns.

8. It is nonetheless a criminal offence to stir up hatred on racial or religious grounds or on the grounds of sexual orientation. Offensive or insulting language may also constitute harassment.

9. In addition to the criminal law, the law provides additional protection against offensive or harassing conduct, including employment, service delivery and education.

10. Public bodies are also subject to particular duties which require them to promote good relations between different communities protected by equality law. This may require them actively to prevent or challenge the use of offensive communication.

26 May 2016

The new blasphemies on campus

The Free Speech University Rankings 2018 *makes for grim reading.*

By Tom Slater

In 1811, Percy Bysshe Shelley was banished from Oxford University for publishing a pamphlet called *The Necessity of Atheism*. His act of heresy was punished by close-minded dons who could brook no dissent. More than two centuries later, there are still blasphemies on campus that students commit at their peril.

Today spiked launches the *Free Speech University Rankings 2018*, our fourth annual analysis of campus censorship in the UK academy, and it makes for grim reading: 55 per cent of the 115 universities and students' unions we survey are this year ranked Red under our traffic-light rankings system, meaning they actively censor speech and ideas.

This marks a dip in Reds from last year. But policies dictating what can and can't be said on campus are still becoming more severe in many areas. A startling 46 per cent of institutions restrict discussion of transgenderism: Leeds Beckett, Newcastle, Imperial and more appear to ban 'transphobic propaganda' outright, while St Andrews, Sussex, Cardiff and others commit themselves to ridding the curriculum of 'transphobic material'.

This is remarkable stuff. In some of our most esteemed universities, supposed citadels of free thinking and scientific endeavour, administrations are demanding that debate about transgenderism be shut down and courses be cleansed of un-PC material. How any course about, say, biology, can coexist with this is unfathomable.

And it's not just in relation to trans issues, that most testy and inflamed subject in politics today. We also found that 48 per cent of institutions have policies which warn against insulting faith groups or offending religious sensibilities. One students' union insists that 'the religious sensibilities of the union's members must be respected'. Shelley must be turning in his grave.

What's more, when it comes to who is being censored on campus, it isn't even just provocateurs, coming to campus to stir up controversy – it's students themselves. Over the past three years, students and/or student groups at 17 campuses have been punished for everything from criticising gay marriage on Facebook to organising a Thatcher vs the Miners themed party.

Starker still, both of those bans were the work of university administrations, rather than students' unions. Campus censorship, you see, isn't just the work of safe space belligerents, blue hair flying in the wind. In fact, while SUs tend to be more extreme in their censorship, in that more of them are ranked Red, the proportion of Red universities has been rising over the past few years, while the proportion of Red students' unions has begun to level off and fall.

There's a good deal of hypocrisy here, too. While, for instance, the University of Cardiff won plaudits in 2015 for pressing ahead with a talk by Germaine Greer, despite protests from students over Greer's 'transphobic' comments about gender, at that very same time it had a policy on its books committing itself to cleansing all curricula of 'transphobic material'. So, many universities don't practise what they preach.

The fracas at the University of the West of England in Bristol on Friday night, in which anti-fascist protesters tried to disrupt a speech by Tory MP Jacob Rees-Mogg, shouting 'no platform for fascists' and scuffling with his supporters, reminds us that student activism remains thoroughly intolerant. And, for the fourth year running, students' unions are far more likely to be ranked Red than universities in our survey. But we can't let universities off the hook.

So, what's to be done about it? Suffice it to say, the plans being drawn up by the newly established Office for Students to fine or otherwise punish universities that censor would only make the problem worse. It's fighting one form of illiberalism with another; as SUs are independent organisations, they wouldn't be touched by such measures; and, even if you somehow prohibited campus authorities from censoring, illiberal activists would merely take matters into their own hands.

The problem here isn't technical – it's cultural. Universities have become so bureaucratised, so estranged from their core mission, that they blithely undermine free speech for the sake of avoiding bad press or keeping a lid on campus protest. Meanwhile, students' unions are run by unrepresentative identitarians who genuinely think words are like bullets.

If we want to change that, we need to change minds. We need to build a culture of free debate and argument so that censorship is no longer enacted so casually. And we need to defeat the patronising argument that censorship must be done for our own good. Students, academics and university leaders need to assert, as Shelley might have put it, the necessity of freedom: the most dangerous idea of all.

5 February 2018

www.spiked-online.com

What you need to know about the new free speech pledge for universities

An article from The Conversation

THE CONVERSATION

By Suzanne Whitten, PhD Philosophy Candidate, Queen's University Belfast

Universities may no longer be able to ban controversial speakers from giving talks on campus – those that continue to do so could face a fine. The freedom to debate and discuss difficult topics should remain a central feature of university life, according to the universities minister, Sam Gyimah.

The new plans come after concerns over 'no-platforming' of controversial speakers, and the censorship of certain viewpoints, which have all led to mounting pressure for government intervention.

To tackle the issue, Gyimah has called for a single clear set of guidelines for both students and institutions to replace the 'dizzying variety' of rules about who can be invited to speak on university campuses and what they can say.

This is the first government intervention on free speech on campus for 30 years. And the new plans could see universities named and shamed or even fined if they don't uphold the rules of free speech.

Tentacles of bureaucracy

Writing in *The Times*, Gyimah echoed recent public concerns about the stifling of free speech on university campuses. Blaming what he referred to as a 'murky' landscape with an array 'of disjointed guidelines'. He noted how those 'unseen and pernicious tentacles of bureaucracy can so often reach out and hold events back'.

Gyimah hopes that the construction of a set of clear guidelines will enhance the landscape of free speech within universities. This will also allow speakers to present their views without the threat of censorship or 'shouting down'.

But Gyimah's concerns over an increasingly bureaucratic university culture also reveal wider problems with the business model of higher education. Increased competition in the graduate job market, combined with rising costs to attend university, has caused a shift in the role of students. Once in the unique position to engage in intellectual curiosity, many young people now approach a university education as a consumer product.

This places pressure on administrators and academics to deliver a particular university 'experience' that fulfils the demands of the consumers themselves. That this phenomenon has led to issues of no-platforming and censorship, then, is no surprise.

Academic freedom

This latest move by the universities minister signals official recognition of the issue of free speech on campus. The introduction of uniform regulations across universities in the UK may offer a welcome level of clarity when navigating such issues.

But, as was revealed in a recent report by the parliamentary joint human rights committee, the potential for over-regulation to contribute to the 'chilling' of free debate should not be ignored. If the government and universities really are committed to securing free speech on campus, difficult questions on the sources of these clashes must not be avoided.

Ministers must also consider the broader problems suffered by academic freedom itself. This means avoiding over-generalised language regarding clashes between the political right-wing and a so-called 'snowflake' culture and instead actually listening to those from all corners of the debate.

Though the temptation to frame the debate in terms of the threat of 'political correctness' remains ever present, this approach is both unhelpful to the furthering of free speech and unnecessarily politically partisan.

Value of higher education

As the first government intervention of its kind since 1986 – when universities became subject to a duty to support freedom of speech – there is hope that the proposed guidance will go some way towards resolving current tensions.

It is believed that recommendations made by the newly formed Office of Students will be considered as possible modes of regulation. But these rules will need to be clearly defined and made transparent, or else risk falling into an even more constrictive state of regulation. This will be no easy feat.

What is needed is a broader approach to the problems of freedom of speech on campus. Providing clear guidance for invited speakers is only one part of the equation. Governments must also strive to ensure that those from all sections of society are given equal opportunity to access higher education. And that those voices are included in the social fabric of university life.

Safeguarding a commitment to academic freedom also requires making sure that academics themselves are adequately valued for both their teaching responsibilities and research contributions. This is important because taken as a symptom of a wider issue in universities today, the free speech debate cannot be separated from these broader concerns about the value of higher education itself.

9 May 2018

Internet censorship: making the hidden visible

Despite being founded on ideals of freedom and openness, censorship on the internet is rampant, with more than 60 countries engaging in some form of state-sponsored censorship. A research project at the University of Cambridge is aiming to uncover the scale of this censorship, and to understand how it affects users and publishers of information

'Censorship over the internet can potentially achieve unprecedented scale'

Sheharbano Khattak

For all the controversy it caused, *Fitna* is not a great film. The 17-minute short, by the Dutch far-right politician Geert Wilders, was a way for him to express his opinion that Islam is an inherently violent religion. Understandably, the rest of the world did not see things the same way. In advance of its release in 2008, the film received widespread condemnation, especially within the Muslim community.

When a trailer for *Fitna* was released on YouTube, authorities in Pakistan demanded that it be removed from the site. YouTube offered to block the video in Pakistan, but would not agree to remove it entirely. When YouTube relayed this decision back to the Pakistan Telecommunications Authority (PTA), the decision was made to block YouTube.

Although Pakistan has been intermittently blocking content since 2006, a more persistent blocking policy was implemented in 2011, when porn content was censored in response to a media report that highlighted Pakistan as the top country in terms of searches for porn. Then, in 2012, YouTube was blocked for three years when a video, deemed

blasphemous, appeared on the website. Only in January this year was the ban lifted, when Google, which owns YouTube, launched a Pakistan-specific version, and introduced a process by which governments can request the blocking of access to offending material.

All of this raises the thorny issue of censorship. Those censoring might raise objections to material on the basis of offensiveness or incitement to violence (more than a dozen people died in Pakistan following widespread protests over the video uploaded to YouTube in 2012). But when users aren't able to access a particular site, they often don't know whether it's because the site is down, or if some force is preventing them from accessing it. How can users know what is being censored and why?

'The goal of a censor is to disrupt the flow of information,' says Sheharbano Khattak, a PhD student in Cambridge's Computer Laboratory, who studies internet censorship and its effects. 'Internet censorship threatens free and open access to information. There's no code of conduct when it comes to censorship: those doing the censoring – usually governments – aren't in the habit of revealing what they're blocking access to.' The goal of her research is to make the hidden visible.

She explains that we haven't got a clear understanding of the consequences of censorship: how it affects different stakeholders, the steps those stakeholders take in response to censorship, how effective an act of censorship is, and what kind of collateral damage it causes.

Because censorship operates in an inherently adversarial environment, gathering relevant datasets is difficult. Much

of the key information, such as what was censored and how, is missing. In her research, Khattak has developed methodologies that enable her to monitor censorship by characterising what normal data looks like and flagging anomalies within the data that are indicative of censorship.

She designs experiments to measure various aspects of censorship, to detect censorship in actively and passively collected data, and to measure how censorship affects various players.

The primary reasons for government-mandated censorship are political, religious or cultural. A censor might take a range of steps to stop the publication of information, to prevent access to that information by disrupting the link between the user and the publisher, or to directly prevent users from accessing that information. But the key point is to stop that information from being disseminated.

Internet censorship takes two main forms: user-side and publisher-side. In user-side censorship, the censor disrupts the link between the user and the publisher. The interruption can be made at various points in the process between a user typing an address into their browser and being served a site on their screen. Users may see a variety of different error messages, depending on what the censor wants them to know.

'The thing is, even in countries like Saudi Arabia, where the government tells people that certain content is censored, how can we be sure of everything they're stopping their citizens from being able to access?' asks Khattak. 'When a government has the power to block access to large parts of the internet, how can we be sure that they're not blocking more than they're letting on?'

What Khattak does is characterise the demand for blocked content and try to work out where it goes. In the case of the blocking of YouTube in 2012 in Pakistan, a lot of the demand went to rival video sites like Daily Motion. But in the case of pornographic material, which is also heavily censored in Pakistan, the government censors didn't have a comprehensive list of sites that were blacklisted, so plenty of pornographic content slipped through the censors' nets.

Despite any government's best efforts, there will always be individuals and publishers who can get around censors, and access or publish blocked content through the use of censorship resistance systems. A desirable property, of any censorship resistance system is to ensure that users are not traceable, but usually users have to combine them with anonymity services such as Tor.

'It's like an arms race, because the technology which is used to retrieve and disseminate information is constantly evolving,' says Khattak. 'We now have social media sites which have loads of user-generated content, so it's very difficult for a censor to retain control of this information because there's so much of it. And because this content is hosted by sites like Google or Twitter that integrate a plethora of services,

wholesale blocking of these websites is not an option most censors might be willing to consider.'

In addition to traditional censorship, Khattak also highlights a new kind of censorship – publisher-side censorship – where websites refuse to offer services to a certain class of users. Specifically, she looks at the differential treatments of Tor users by some parts of the web. The issue with services like Tor is that visitors to a website are anonymised, so the owner of the website doesn't know where their visitors are coming from. There is increasing use of publisher-side censorship from site owners who want to block users of Tor or other anonymising systems.

'Censorship is not a new thing,' says Khattak. 'Those in power have used censorship to suppress speech or writings deemed objectionable for as long as human discourse has existed. However, censorship over the internet can potentially achieve unprecedented scale, while possibly remaining discrete so that users are not even aware that they are being subjected to censored information.'

Professor Jon Crowcroft, who Khattak works with, agrees: 'It's often said that, online, we live in an echo chamber, where we hear only things we agree with. This is a side of the filter bubble that has its flaws, but is our own choosing. The darker side is when someone else gets to determine what we see, despite our interests. This is why internet censorship is so concerning.'

'While the cat and mouse game between the censors and their opponents will probably always exist,' says Khattak. 'I hope that studies such as mine will illuminate and bring more transparency to this opaque and complex subject, and inform policy around the legality and ethics of such practices.'

14 October 2016

www.cam.ac.uk

Which countries censor the internet today?

Depending on where you live, free and open access to the information and entertainment found on the internet might seem like more of a right than a privilege. But for folks who live in some of the world's more restrictive societies, some or even most of the internet remains tantalisingly out of reach, blocked by government censors and their firewalls.

Reasons for censorship

The majority of such internet censorship is employed in the name of combating software piracy and other types of illegal file sharing (including torrents and file hosting sites such as New Zealand's controversial Mega.co.nz). It's interesting to note, however, that while such traffic is actively condemned by both governments and intellectual property advocates alike, corporations such as Netflix are using torrent activity to help them plan their own (legal) offerings.

Another justification for widespread censorship and monitoring of legal content (including torrents, political and social media, and yes, pornography) is state-enforced morality. Countries engaged in this sort of censorship often claim to be looking out for the welfare of their citizenry, but critics are quick to point out that the countries with the most censorship are often the same ones with a history of aggressively suppressing public protest or political unrest.

If you're taking a trip around the world and plan on accessing the internet (including basics such as email and social media) while you're on the road, you may need to review and adjust your itinerary if it includes heavily-censored countries such as Eritrea, China, Somalia, or the famously secretive and regulated North Korea. Torrent users – even those who rely on the embattled tech to share legitimate, legal files – might find themselves out of luck no matter where they go.

How censorship might affect your life

It's not just moral or intellectual outrage that's driving censorship, of course. With the issue of net neutrality dominating news in the tech sector, the spectre of another form of censorship – selective or restricted access based on corporate policies, as compared to government intervention – has reared its troubling head.

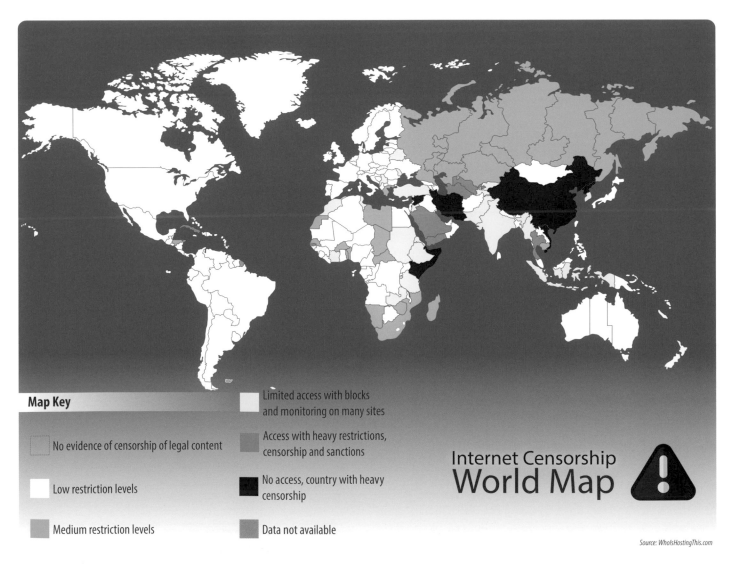

Map Key

☐ No evidence of censorship of legal content

☐ Low restriction levels

☐ Medium restriction levels

☐ Limited access with blocks and monitoring on many sites

☐ Access with heavy restrictions, censorship and sanctions

☐ No access, country with heavy censorship

☐ Data not available

Internet Censorship
World Map ⚠

Country	Social media	Pornography	Political media	Country	Social media	Pornography	Political media	Country	Social media	Pornography	Political media
Asia				Turkmenistan				Peru			
Afghanistan				UAE (United Arab Emirates)				Venezuela			
Armenia				Uzbekistan				**Europe**			
Azerbaijan				Vietnam				Austria			
Bahrain				Yemen				Belarus			
Bangladesh				**Africa**				Belgium			
Burma/Myanmar				Algeria				Bulgaria			
Cambodia				Angola				Croatia			
China				Egypt				Czech Republic			
Cyprus				Eritrea				Denmark			
Gaza Strip				Ethiopia				Estonia			
Georgia				Gambia, The				Finland			
India				Ghana				France			
Indonesia				Kenya				Germany			
Iran				Libya				Greece			
Iraq				Malawi				Hungary			
Israel				Mauritania				Iceland			
Japan				Morocco				Ireland			
Jordan				Nigeria				Isle of Man			
Kazakhstan				Rwanda				Italy			
Korea, North				South Africa				Latvia			
Korea, South				Sudan				Moldova			
Kuwait				Swaziland				Netherlands			
Kyrgyzstan				Tunisia				Norway			
Laos				Uganda				Poland			
Lebanon				**North America**				Portugal			
Malaysia				Bahamas, The				Romania			
Mongolia				Canada				Russia			
Nepal				Cuba				Slovakia			
Oman				Guatemala				Slovenia			
Pakistan				Mexico				Spain			
Philippines				United States				Sweden			
Qatar				**South America**				Switzerland			
Saudi Arabia				Argentina				Turkey			
Singapore				Brazil				Ukraine			
Sri Lanka				Chile				United Kingdom			
Syria				Colombia				**Australia**			
Tajikistan				Ecuador				Australia			
Thailand				Paraguay				Fiji			
								New Zealand			

All countries have limited access with blocks and monitoring on torrents, except North Korea which has no access.

- No evidence of censorship of legal content
- 'Default On' – content censored unless access requested
- Limited access with blocks and monitoring on many sites
- Access with heavy restrictions, censorship, and sanctions
- No access
- *Country* Country with heavy censorship

Source: WhoIsHostingThis.com

Regardless of the form, it's clear that equal and open access to the internet is something no one can afford to take for granted any longer, and that the discussion of how much – if any – of the internet can or should be censored will continue far into the future.

The internet, and our freedom to use it as we please, is a contentious issue. Whereas access in some countries can be unrestricted for any materials its government deign legal, in others censorship ranges from governments blocking the dissemination of political opinion, to blacklisting pornographic and social media websites.

Most democratic countries have little Internet censorship, mainly to control piracy. However, some countries limit access to information and suppress discussion among citizens, often in anticipation of elections, protests and riots.

Freedom of the Internet is not a guarantee.

22 April 2018

www.whoishostingthis.com

The technology of censorship

The internet and the world wide web once held a revolutionary promise for good.

By Dickon Ross

The technologists were idealistic about it: information wants to be free, they said, and so it would be. The internet was originally designed to withstand a nuclear strike, so it could certainly withstand a roadblock. If anyone tried to block information going by one route, it would simply find another way. The internet would democratise, empower, expose and, in the process, the truth would come out. It would be the end of censorship because it would become impossible.

That was only a couple of decades ago, but that vision now seems like an impossible dream. Countries have discovered they can pretty effectively limit internet activity – or at least make it difficult for most of their population. Not only that, they can interfere to provide their version of the truth in other jurisdictions beyond their own.

Not all censorship is bad. Few people are complete libertarians. When material online incites hatred, violence or criminality, for example, most people would support stopping it, even in our liberal democracies. Every society censors something, but some censor a lot more than others.

While the social media networks find themselves subject to censorship, sometimes it is the networks themselves that act as the censors, and Paul Dempsey asks if they are getting any better at making the right decisions.

Many of us act as censors for our children – or perhaps should do if we don't. Parents are the censors that teenagers most worry about. Age restrictions are easily circumvented. It's easy to lie about your age, but Tim Fryer finds out how that could all change with new age verification technology. Perhaps households should be careful what they are saying too? Martin Courtney looks at how voice-activated digital assistants in the home could be recording our every word if we're not careful.

Censorship goes hand in hand with surveillance. In an exclusive investigation, Josh Loeb finds out how the good guys are using advanced technology to keep an eye on the bad guys. He discovers the UK police is well advanced in face recognition technology yet is using only a fraction of its capabilities.

Internet communication isn't the only data open to interference. Ships off the coast of Russia have found their GPS telling them they are in an airport. Spoofing GPS is more dangerous than jamming it and Hilary Clarke finds out where it's happening and why, while our very own Vitali Vitaliev recalls censorship and jamming in the Soviet Union long before the days of the internet, Facebook and GPS. Censorship, it seems, will always find a way.

12 October 2017

eandt.theiet.org

The rise of social media censorship

A blog by Emma Davies

Social media: love it or loath it, it is here to stay, or is it? The evolution of social media has been a monumental boost for public self-expression. With roughly 36% of the world's population owning a social media account, political regimes and cultures that do not uphold the principle of freedom of speech are becoming increasingly threatened by the power of social media to influence, giving rise to endless arrests, detentions, internet shutdowns and social media taxes.

Southern Iraq

Earlier this month people in Southern Iraq were protesting over high unemployment rates and poor infrastructure.

Just before the security forces used live fire and tear gas to control what was only a peaceful protest, the government cut the internet. Protesters were not able to post images and videos of the unnecessary violence being used. A source in Baghdad told us:

'When there is no internet, people are being beaten and killed because we can't upload it. Iraqis now know the value of social media. We need it to raise our voice.'

Iran

Many Iranian women have been detained for posting so called 'indecent' clips or images on their Instagram accounts. Police say that they are 'damaging public virtue through the organised spreading of anti-cultural' activities.

These crackdowns are fast becoming a regular activity to control Western cultural influence. The women who have been detained are mainly photographers, models, dancers, wedding and beauty industry professionals and lifestyle bloggers who use the platform to promote their work.

Dancing

Maedeh Hojabri, is an 18-year-old gymnast and dancer, who was arrested for posting clips of herself performing dance routines on Instagram. She 'confessed' on state TV to 'breaking moral norms' by posting the clip.

Another dance incident was that of a Saudi teenager who was filmed dancing to 90's favourite, 'Macarena' on a street crossing. The clip went viral and the teenager was detained for 'improper public behaviour'.

Egypt

Egyptian human rights activist, and mother Amal Fathy has been arrested for sharing her experience of sexual harassment on Facebook.

Amal was arrested in May 2018 for posting a video on Facebook condemning sexual harassment and criticising the Egyptian government for their inaction on this issue.

Uganda

The Ugandan government has introduced a 5% tax on social media usage. People protesting the tax in Kumpala have been met with violent oppression from the police, including tear gas and live fire. According to Frank Tumwebaze, Uganda's ICT Minister, the money raised will be used to 'invest in more broadband infrastructure'. However, the reasons for the tax are blurry, President Yoweri Museveni justified the charge saying many Ugandans did not pay enough tax and should not 'donate money to foreign companies through chatting or even lying' on social media.

Our regional director for the area Joan Nyanyuki responded to the tax saying that it is:

'A clear attempt to undermine the right to freedom of expression' and that 'by making people pay for using these platforms, this tax will render these avenues of communication inaccessible for low income earners, robbing many people of their right to freedom of expression, with a chilling effect on other human rights'.

Algeria

In January 2017 Algeria-based blogger Merzoug Touati was arrested and charged with 'encouraging civil unrest' simply for posting his opinion on Facebook and Youtube. He faced a possible death sentence. After 18 months in detention he was sentenced to ten years imprisonment.

Heba Morayef, Middle East and North Africa Regional Director at Amnesty International, said:

'Merzoug Touati's arrest, trial and sentence is further proof that freedom of expression remains under threat in Algeria, where the authorities continue to use a range of repressive laws to quell dissent.'

26 July 2018

Freedom of the press

Chapter 2

UK among the worst in western Europe for press freedom

Latest global ranking places Britain behind Uruguay, Samoa and Chile for restrictions on reporters.

By Jim Waterson, Media editor

The UK has one of the worst environments for press freedom in western Europe, according to a global ranking that places Britain below the likes of Uruguay, Samoa, and Chile for restrictions on reporters as they seek to hold power to account.

Reporters Without Borders, which campaigns for journalistic freedoms, said the UK ranked 40th out of 180 countries on its annual *World Press Freedom Index*, leaving it ranked between Trinidad & Tobago and Burkina Faso.

The campaigning organisation cited proposals to introduce tougher press regulation, the government's campaign to limit encryption on services such as WhatsApp, and restrictions by Labour and the Conservatives on journalists' access to politicians during the 2017 general election as evidence of a 'heavy-handed' approach towards the media in the UK.

Other concerns include law firm Appleby using British courts to sue *The Guardian* and the BBC over the publication of the

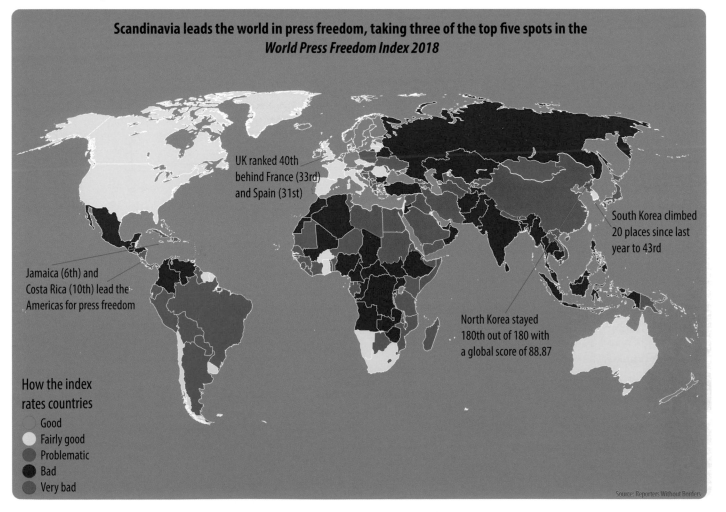

Scandinavia leads the world in press freedom, taking three of the top five spots in the *World Press Freedom Index 2018*

UK ranked 40th behind France (33rd) and Spain (31st)

South Korea climbed 20 places since last year to 43rd

Jamaica (6th) and Costa Rica (10th) lead the Americas for press freedom

North Korea stayed 180th out of 180 with a global score of 88.87

How the index rates countries
- Good
- Fairly good
- Problematic
- Bad
- Very bad

Source: Reporters Without Borders

The Guardian editor, Katharine Viner, launched the report at The Guardian's office in central London, warning the worldwide 'situation in terms of press freedom is getting worse'. She said journalists should not forget to campaign for press freedom in the UK, in addition to other countries.

James Harding, who until recently was in charge of the BBC's news operation, said that while misinformation on social media was widely discussed it was often the actions of governments that caused real damage.

'For all the discussion of fake news, there is the much more pervasive problem of state news, which is the problem of governments and politicians encroaching on the media,' he said.

They were joined by reporter Matthew Caruana Galizia, the son of murdered Maltese journalist Daphne Caruana Galizia, who said the public should be aware that even in Europe journalists were being killed as a result of their work.

Paradise Papers, plus the fact the BBC political editor, Laura Kuenssberg, required a bodyguard for her protection while attending last autumn's political party conferences.

Reporters Without Borders' UK bureau director, Rebecca Vincent, said Britain's ranking was 'unacceptable for a country that plays an important international standard-setting role when it comes to human rights and fundamental freedoms'.

'We must examine the longer-term trend of worrying moves to restrict press, and hold the government to account,' she added.

Scandinavian countries scored highest on the list, with Norway taking top spot. Italy was the only western European country to have a lower ranking than the UK.

Canada ranked 18th, Australia was 19th, while the US came in at 45th. New Zealand gained five places to rank eighth.

'Her murder has really resulted in a national trauma that is going to take us decades to recover from,' he said. 'There is no one who has stepped up to claim that spot and continue the fight that she was fighting.'

He urged others to step up and continue her work. 'It was easy for the people she was reporting on – all they had to do was eliminate her and they thought that would eliminate the story.'

25 April 2018

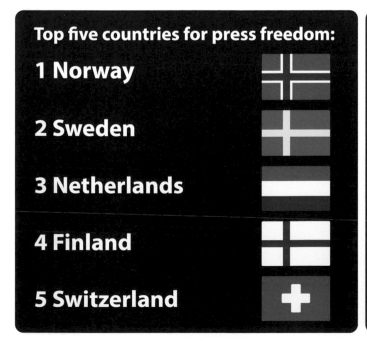

Top five countries for press freedom:

1 Norway

2 Sweden

3 Netherlands

4 Finland

5 Switzerland

Worst five countries for press freedom:

176 China

177 Syria

178 Turkmenistan

179 Eritrea

180 North Korea

Press freedom: getting darker

Journalism is under attack across the world – including the UK.

By Katharine Quarmby

Britain leads the way in Europe - but not in a good way. It has a worse record on press freedom than all other European nation states except Italy, trailing others such as Norway, Sweden and the Netherlands.

In the *2018 World Press Freedom Index*, an annual report, by Reporters Without Borders (RSF), Britain was judged to have been in 40th place. This compared to Norway and Sweden at the top of the index, with the UK coming in below Trinidad and Tobago and only just ahead of Taiwan. The United States is also trailing, to the dismay of American media organisations, coming in at 45 on the list (with North Korea in bottom place, at 180).

'A continued heavy-handed approach towards the press... has resulted in the UK keeping its status as one of the worst-ranked Western European countries'

RSF has drawn attention to several issues that may have contributed to Britain's place in the ranking. It says: 'A continued heavy-handed approach towards the press (often in the name of national security) has resulted in the UK keeping its status as one of the worst-ranked Western European countries in the World Press Freedom Index.'

It points, in particular, to online threats against journalists, many of them women, proposed changes to the Official Secrets Act, repeated attempts to impose state-backed press regulation – and a legal action by the law firm, Appleby, against *The Guardian* and the BBC, for work on the Paradise Papers. The UK is the only place where such proceedings have started in the wake of international revelations over tax avoidance.

The UK's poor ranking has drawn reactions from freedom of expression organisations.

'It's depressing that the UK has maintained its recent low ranking in the World Press Freedom Index', said Jodie Ginsberg, Chief Executive of Index on Censorship, a body campaigning for freedom of expression. She added: 'The environment for press freedom is declining globally and we need to see leaders speak out more in its defence. Instead we see the likes of Donald Trump smearing anyone who criticises him as a peddler of "fake news". This does little to promote the central value of press freedom, as a cornerstone of democracy, around the world – and in fact emboldens those in positions of power everywhere to suppress further journalists and journalism.'

'My reporting means that I cannot go back whilst it is ruled by a regime which targets journalists and their families.'

So what does this mean for us, as journalists working in the public interest? As Index on Censorship says, about its project to map media freedom, journalists and media workers are confronting relentless pressure simply for doing their job.

A straw poll of journalists in the Bureau itself demonstrates that restrictions on press freedom have impacted on work and reduced our capacity to tell stories that matter, both in the UK and abroad.

My own work has been affected, in the UK and in Iran, where family members live. One of my books, *Hear My Cry*, on 'honour' violence affecting a British-Yemen citizen, has had to be published elsewhere in the EU, as potential publishers here were concerned about the weak safeguards for public interest journalism here under the Defamation Act.

When I visited family in Iran in 2007, under the Ahmadinejad regime, I travelled to the country on a tourist visa, rather than a journalist visa, as I knew that I could then meet family members and friends without a minder present. As my Iranian birth father, like many other naval officers, had been imprisoned after the Revolution it would have been risky for him to meet me if I was under constant surveillance. When I returned to the UK, I did write and broadcast on my experiences in Iran. But I am aware that it would be problematic to go back now, as the current regime targets journalists – and their families, if they have Iranian connections. I would be putting myself and my Iranian birth family at risk. Iran was ranked at 164 on this year's press freedom list.

The Bureau itself, with other organisations supporting freedom of expression, currently has a case at the European Court of Human Rights, about which our managing editor, Rachel Oldroyd, has written. The Bureau brought the case in 2014, with the aim of forcing the government to provide adequate protections and safeguards for journalists' privileged communications. Without these protections, we argued, the government's actions were a direct threat to a free press and indirectly would have a chilling effect on whistleblowers seeking to expose wrongdoing. In November 2017 the arguments were made in a rare aural hearing at the court, combined with two other cases brought by a group of human rights organisations including Amnesty International, Privacy International and Liberty. The case is currently being considered.

'I was deported by the Israeli authorities... banned from Israel and therefore from visiting Palestine, for ten years'

Jessica Purkiss, one of the Bureau's foreign affairs reporters, has also faced difficulties. She says: 'While reporting on issues in Palestine I was deported by the Israeli authorities. Israel controls the borders to Palestine so entrance depends

on their approval. The security personnel were clear to tell me that I was not being deported for being a journalist but for taking a photo of a Palestinian protest – something that was not illegal to my knowledge – which they had obtained by going through my computer. After a night in a detention cell, I was escorted onto a plane back to the UK and my passport withheld until I landed on British soil. I have been banned from Israel, and therefore from visiting Palestine, for ten years.' She has also faced problems in Palestine: 'During my time in Palestine I wrote a story about the poor treatment of teenagers arrested by the Palestinian Authority. I received a call from their press office informing me that if I didn't provide the names and addresses of the children, I could face charges of withholding evidence.' Israel was ranked at 87 on this year's list and Palestine at 134.

'We need a US First Amendment-style law, which guarantees freedom of the press'

Meirion Jones, our investigations editor, has also encountered difficulties in his long career in journalism.

Just this week one of the British fraudsters who sold fake bomb detectors to Iraq was given two more years prison time under proceeds of crime legislation because he wouldn't surrender some of the millions of pounds he made from his crime.

The fraud, which probably cost the lives of 2,000 Iraqis who were blown up after the detectors failed to detect explosives, was uncovered by a team led by the Bureau's Investigations Editor Meirion Jones when he was at BBC *Newsnight*. But Jones believes a major reason that the fraudsters set up business in the UK was because the libel laws made it so difficult to expose them: 'One of the bogus bomb detector makers hired extremely expensive lawyers to threaten to sue us for libel if we said the detectors were fake', he said.

He also did the original investigation into the paedophile Jimmy Savile: 'Savile was protected for years by British libel law and lawyers, including the late George Carman QC. Many in the British press knew or suspected Savile was a paedophile for decades but were too afraid of being sued for millions to tell the truth - we need a US First Amendment style law which guarantees freedom of the press.'

Our Afghan expert, Payenda Sargand, faced an uncomfortable experience in Dubai. 'I was detained for taking the photo of a plain commercial building in Dubai in 2003. The police detained me and confiscated my camera after they spotted me getting ready to take a photo of Emirates Towers [a building complex in Dubai]. I explained to them that I was a journalist and I had not yet even taken a picture of the towers. Their argument was that it was illegal to take pictures of the complex. They took me to a police station and kept me for over eight hours, under a freezing air conditioner. Their behaviour was unprofessional and rude. I have tried to find out more about this ever since. I believe the only reason for my detention was to do with the fact that I am Afghan. It didn't matter that I was a journalist.' The United Arab Emirates is 128 on the world ranking.

Another Bureau journalist, whose experience is anonymised to protect the source, had problems in Vietnam (ranked this year at 175). 'While trying to partner on a sensitive subject I was assigned a press minder. On the one day I tried to report on my own I received an anonymous text message, warning me that the police would be waiting for me if I travelled to meet my source. In fear for my source I cancelled the meeting and managed to get the story another way.'

Most chillingly, of course, is the fact that journalists die every year because of their work in war-zones, unmasking corruption and speaking truth to power, most recently the Cypriot journalist, Daphne Caruana Galizia. Journalism is not a crime - but reading the World Press Freedom Index this year, you would be forgiven for thinking that it is all too often seen as one.

27 April 2018

www.thebureauinvestigates.com

A free press is fundamental to a mature society – but the press is not infallible

By Simon Kelner

For those of us worried about the regulation and freedom of the press – which should be all of us – there have been two interesting developments this week.

First, *The Times* published a ruling by the Independent Press Standards Organisation (IPSO), criticising the newspaper's 'distorted' report over fostering arrangements in the east London borough of Tower Hamlets. Second, came the publication of a report which put the UK in 40th place in the world for press freedoms, slightly above Burkina Faso but below Estonia.

There may appear no direct relation between these two pieces of news, but they are, in my view, connected. Six years ago, just before Lord Leveson's inquiry into the 'culture and practices and ethics' of the British press, the UK was 12 places higher in the World Press Freedom Index.

'The Data Protection Bill will have a chilling effect on investigative journalism'

The Leveson Inquiry was commissioned as a reaction to public outrage over the excesses of British newspapers, with particular reference to the phone-hacking scandal. As a result, the newspapers set up a self-regulatory body, the IPSO. It was its ruling that *The Times* felt obliged to put on its own front page, and page two. In this narrow case, at least, you could argue that self-regulation of the press works.

Exposure

But in the wake of Leveson, other forces were at work, which would also explain why the UK has fallen so dramatically in the Press Freedom Index. There is little doubt that the lives of some rich, famous and powerful people would be made a good deal easier if the freedoms of journalists to investigate their affairs were curtailed. The Leveson Inquiry, and some of the heinous activities of British newspapers that it exposed, offered them the legitimacy to support authoritarian legislation, which is an impediment to investigative journalism.

This is what is reflected in the World Press Freedom Index. I am not saying that those who oppose the current arrangements are merely self-interested, but I think that, on a finely balanced issue, they fall in the wrong side. The ability of newspapers to hold the mighty to account is one of the fundamentals of a mature democracy such as ours, and should be protected at the risk of isolated episodes of bad behaviour by newspapers.

Before Lord Leveson's inquiry the UK was 12 places higher in the World Press Freedom Index

The World Press Freedom Index is instructive in that it points out where the pendulum in the UK has swung in a way that is counter to the interests of the wider public. The Data Protection Bill, reforms to the Official Secrets Act, and the introduction of Section 40 of the Crime and Courts Act, will all have a chilling effect on investigative journalism.

This is not just a case of special pleading: these are very real threats to the willingness of whistle-blowers to come forward, to the ability of journalists to access hidden data, and the inclination of newspapers, already under huge financial pressures, to print the information.

This, I accept, is not a top priority for average citizens. We can only hope that the publication of an index which shows Britain to be the worst country in western Europe for press freedom will get their attention.

25 April 2018

How deadly has 2018 been for journalists?

Reporters around the world are facing growing threats of violence, according to campaigners.

By Tom Parfitt

Viktoria Marinova, a Bulgarian journalist, was found raped and murdered in a park on Saturday. The television presenter had recently covered a story about the suspected misuse of EU funds by businesses. The 30-year-old is the third journalist to have been murdered in Europe in the past year, following other fatal attacks on investigative reporters in Malta and Slovakia.

The killings have led campaigners to warn that press freedom on the continent is in danger, as journalists face growing threats, intimidation and violence, in Europe and around the world.

And last week, Saudi Arabian dissident and *Washington Post* journalist Jamal Khashoggi disappeared after entering the Saudi embassy in Istanbul. His disappearance sparked concern among Turkish officials that the 59-year-old had been killed inside the consulate, although this has been denied by the Saudi government, who maintain that he left the building. Mr Khashoggi has lived in self-imposed exile in Washington for the past year fearing retribution for his critical views on Saudi policies.

How many journalists have been killed so far in 2018?

According to the Committee to Protect Journalists (CPJ), a New York based organisation defending the freedom of the press, at least 43 journalists have been killed in 2018 so far. The figure includes those who died in the line of fire while covering conflicts or on dangerous assignments, as well as those who were murdered. Russian journalists Alexander Rastorguyev, Kirill Radchenko and Orkhan Dzhemal were killed in June while working on a story in the Central African Republic.

How many journalists were killed in 2017?

Figures released by the CPJ show that 46 journalists were killed in 2017. The victims included Daphne Caruana Galizia, a prominent investigative reporter in Malta, who was killed in a car bombing last October. Ms Caruana Galizia, who ran a blog titled *Running Commentary*, had written reports about the Panama Papers tax avoidance scandal. Slovakian journalist Jan Kuciak and his fiancée Martina Kusnirova were shot dead at their home outside Bratislava last February. Mr Kuciak had reported on Slovakian businessmen mentioned in the Panama Papers leak.

What were the deadliest years for journalists?

Since the CPJ's records began in 1992, 2009 was the deadliest year for journalists, with 76 journalists killed worldwide. A total of 74 were killed in 2012, making it the second deadliest year, while 73 were killed in 2015.

Which countries are most dangerous for journalists?

The most dangerous countries for journalists are Afghanistan, Syria, Mexico and Iraq, according to the non-profit group Reporters Without Borders. At least 12 journalists have been killed so far in Afghanistan this year, the CPJ said, with nine of them murdered in twin bomb attacks in Kabul in April.

What is causing the rise in journalist deaths?

Long-running conflicts in Afghanistan, Syria and Iraq mean that journalists on the frontline often face being caught in the line of fire. Of the countries not at war, Mexico is the most dangerous for reporters because powerful drug cartels increasingly target journalists who expose organised crime. According to the CPJ, 47 journalists in the North American country have been killed since 1992, with four of these killings taking place this year.

9 October 2018

Global crackdown on fake news raises censorship concerns

Hastily drawn-up measures outlawing false or misleading information may prove counterproductive, campaigners say.

By Jon Henley

In a world where false and misleading information reaches billions instantly and online manipulation is becoming ever more sophisticated, governments are increasingly turning to legislation to combat fake news.

But unlike, say, hate speech, terrorism advocacy or child pornography, fake news is a tricky area for the law: it has not, generally, been illegal – and in democracies, political speech is seen as deserving the strongest of free speech protections.

Lawyers, technology experts, media representatives and free speech campaigners have expressed fears that hastily drawn-up domestic measures outlawing fake news may at best prove ineffective, and at worst counterproductive.

'All too often, legislation focuses on the trees, not the forest,' said Alberto Alemanno, a professor of EU law. 'It's quite likely to end up being irrelevant, or even to exacerbate the root causes of the fake news phenomenon.'

Infinitely easier and cheaper to produce and spread than ever before, fake news is also 'low-hanging fruit' for politicians, Alemanno said: 'They can talk to voters about it, whereas tackling the underlying, structural reasons why it's so pervasive in our society and media environment is far, far harder.'

From Europe to Asia, leaders are rushing to adopt anti-fake news laws. France – where 'fake news', necessarily narrowly defined so as to protect free speech, has been illegal since 1881 – aims to allow judges to order the deletion of false online content in election periods.

The legislation will also oblige social media platforms to name advertisers who are financing content, and say how much they are paying, and permit France's independent broadcasting authority to suspend media seen as trying to destabilise a vote, notably if 'influenced by foreigners'.

Germany earlier this year also introduced an online hate speech law, giving platforms with more than two million users 24 hours to remove 'obviously illegal' terror content, racist material and fake news or face fines of up to €50million (£44milliont). Other offensive material must be blocked within seven days.

Other EU countries including Sweden, Ireland and the Czech Republic are weighing or implementing anti-fake news legislations. But as campaigners warn such laws could curb free speech or lead to inadvertent censorship, regimes often highly sensitive to media criticism stand accused of using similar legislation to try to silence free expression and opposition groups.

Criticised for mounting a 'full-frontal assault on mainstream journalism', India last month abruptly withdrew, 24 hours after it was unveiled, a sweeping new order allowing the suspension of any journalist so much as suspected of spreading fake news (which it did not define).

But Malaysia has passed a law setting fines of up to £88,000 and jail terms of up to six years for offenders who use traditional news outlets, digital publications and social media – including outside Malaysia – to spread fake news. Opponents have said the law takes the country 'one step closer to a dictatorship'.

Thailand, too, has a cybersecurity law making the spread of false information liable to a jail term of up to seven years, while Singapore is preparing a report on measures to counter 'deliberate online falsehoods' and the Philippines is mulling anti-fake news legislation that would punish offenders with up to 20 years in jail.

Besides legislation, civil society measures being increasingly adopted to counter fake news, including fact-checking and debunking, also may not ultimately prove effective, Alemanno said. 'The problem here is simply that fact-checkers don't step in until after publication, by which time it's too late.'

Lisa-Maria Neudert of the Oxford Internet Institute, who specialises in countermeasures to computational propaganda, agreed: 'Will a fact-checked story simply increase the visibility of the original? Will it be seen by the same people? Will it be believed? There's a credibility problem. People don't necessarily believe mainstream media and political elites.'

With partners, the media freedom watchdog Reporters sans Frontières has launched the Journalism Trust Initiative, a possible future certification system that would promote rigorous and reliable journalism through standards covering transparency and trust issues such as ownership, independence, revenue sources, journalistic methods and compliance with ethical norms.

'Two once-distinct arenas – the media and public debate – have merged and changed,' said RSF's director, Christophe Deloire. 'False and reliable information now circulates in the same channels, and "bad" news circulates faster than "good". We have to give a real advantage to those who produce reliable journalism.'

Deloire said he was not opposed to 'a good balance between self-regulation and regulation'. But as the EU prepares to unveil a plan for voluntary self-regulation by internet giants

such as Facebook, Twitter and Google, with the threat of laws to follow if they fail to comply, experts doubt that simply demanding the platforms take responsibility is a long-term solution.

'There are questions around the time and resources social networks will put in to do that job, and also whether they are necessarily the best judges of the material,' said Neudert. 'In France, decisions will be made by judges on a case-by-case basis, so there will at least be juridical oversight.

But there are obviously gaps, and it's very hard to see how it will work... Extending existing laws and definitions into the online sphere can be difficult. And now authoritarian regimes can point to democracies taking these steps.'

Alemanno said a big part of the problem was the social media platforms' business model. 'The push has to come from the platforms, but the way they make their money – increasing reader engagement, and monetising their data – means they have no incentive to play the role of arbiters of truth,' he said.

'That may change, eventually. But rather than top-down, prescriptive laws, we should be thinking about changing the environment in which readers act, and empowering them: displaying related, fact-checked articles next to disputed stories; apps allowing users to check for veracity; certification systems.'

For Naudert, the platforms are slowly 'shifting their thinking', realising that a pay-per-click model may not be the best guarantee of their long-term success. 'What's needed most,' she said, 'is more transparency, all round. This is a societal, media and technological problem. Pointing the finger at just one actor won't help.'

24 April 2018

Fake news has always existed, but quality journalism has a history of survival

An article from The Conversation

THE CONVERSATION

By Jackie Harrison, Professor of Public Communication, University of Sheffield

Donald Trump's insistence that any challenges to the actions and utterances of the president are 'fake news' is particularly chilling because it resembles a tactic used by authoritarian regimes seeking ways to silence independent reporting.

Malaysian authorities looking for new ways to criminalise critical news reporting now include fake news charges. In Egypt – dubbed 'one of the world's biggest prisons for journalists' by the Committee to Protect Journalists – being accused of spreading fake news can come with serious sanctions for national news journalists. In March 2018, it was an accusation used increasingly as a means to intimidate and deter foreign media in the run up to the presidential election.

While attempts to diminish the civil standing of journalism within the US has not led to censorship by bullet (though there are reports of attacks and arrests of journalists, exclusion from press calls and seizure of equipment), they are still destructive in their intention to undermine the crucial playing out of dissent and agreement within the civil sphere. Obstructing independent and dissenting journalism is a serious problem in an era where a growing number of news providers see their audiences as partisans rather than citizens.

Audiences who invest in highly partisan news that disconnects itself from truth telling, objectivity and investigative rigour respond positively to the endless pledges of loyalty by news providers, which in turn generate trust from them. These news providers seek to represent and confirm rather than challenge their audience's beliefs and values. Such is the diminishment of public discourse and the proliferation of what author of the 2017 study *Post Truth*, Matthew D'Ancona calls 'incommensurable realities', where 'prudent conduct consists in choosing sides rather than evaluating evidence'.

These days the scale and speed of the way highly partisan news and falsehoods circulate is unprecedented. So far the evidence in the USA has suggested that it is mainly pro-Trump supporters that visit fake news sites.

In his new book *The People vs Democracy*, political theorist Yascha Mounk warns that the populists who have exploited new technology effectively and without constraint have 'been willing to say anything to get elected – to lie to obfuscate and to incite hatred'.

Equally ominous are the findings of an MIT study which noted that resistance to bias and fakery requires real effort, simply because there is a huge appetite for news that is fun, accessible, that reinforces prejudices, is easy to consume and is amusing to share. And while 'robots accelerated the spread of true and false news at the same rate… false news spreads more than the truth because humans, not robots, are more likely to spread it'. Or as a story in the *Atlantic* put it: *Falsehoods almost always beat out the truth on Twitter, penetrating further, faster and deeper into the social network than accurate information… [perhaps because] false stories inspired fear, disgust, and surprise… [while] true stories inspired anticipation, sadness, joy, and trust.*

Partisan and fake news is nothing if not exciting.

A history of survival

For many it's beginning to seem as if fake news is more of a threat than ever and that 'the bad' seems to be edging ahead – but so far it hasn't won. Quality journalism still displays 'civil resistance' and a history of survival is on its side.

The historical reality is that news providers who try to provide truth-telling news have always done so in a hostile climate. And how toxic it is, is just a matter of degrees. Benign and malign news is unchanging in its coexistence, disagreement and fundamental rivalry.

What remains true then and now is how fraudulent news activities succeed so well in engaging their audiences, being shared and recycled in no small part because they so destructively masquerade as genuine news. Truthful news was just as difficult to verify in the era of the invention of the Gutenberg printing press.

As author Kenan Malik points out, in 1672 Charles II had to issue a proclamation 'to restrain the spreading of false news'. In Germany the word 'Lügenpresse' (lying press) has been used as a political insult by both right and left since the mid-19th century and has been employed as an anti-democratic slogan and a xenophobic slur.

Almost a century later in 1931, Stanley Baldwin (then UK prime minister) said of Lord Beaverbrook and Lord Rothermere, proprietors of the *Daily Express* and *Daily Mail*, respectively, that their newspapers employed 'direct falsehoods, misrepresentation, half-truths, the alteration of the speaker's meaning by publishing a sentence apart from the context'.

Nevertheless quality journalism has a history of survival. Why? Because the public, according to most audience surveys, persistently value accurate, sincere and objective news – news that they believe displays editorial integrity. And they do so because they conform to a deeply held need for a fair-minded and comprehensive understanding of events. In other words, the public regard quality journalism as a civil necessity.

The coexistence in the media of what is regarded as desirable and undesirable is inevitable and inescapable. Journalism that is uncomfortable, truthful, critical and interpretative does so because it has a civil disposition. We need it. And this, as ever, is what is at risk.

3 May 2018

New initiative to help children identify fake news welcome addition to on-going digital resilience debate

By Anne Longfield, Children's Commissioner for England

The BBC's new initiative to help secondary school children identify real news and spot fake news could be a game-changing tool for helping children navigate their way through the digital world.

I know from speaking to children myself that they are often more savvy about what they see on the internet and social media than perhaps many adults might think. A recent National Literacy Trust study backs that up. It found that while one in five children believe everything they read online is true, four in five do not. It's clear many secondary school children have already developed a healthy scepticism about what they see and read online. Yet at the same time, the sheer volume of online content, real and fake, that many children are bombarded with grows ever bigger.

We now live in a world where rumour and untruth, disguised as fact, can travel around the globe literally at the click of a button. All of us, even adults, are often unsure what is true and what isn't – and it's unlikely the 'fake news' trend will be just a passing phase. As something that could be part and parcel of the digital lives all of us, it's vital we teach children from an early age that not everything they see online can be trusted.

Of course, that doesn't mean we should be spoon-feeding uncritical children 'mainstream' news and expecting them not to question what they're being told. Even some stories from 'mainstream' platforms could have been produced by people with their own distinctive agendas. It is actually about making sure children are given the opportunities and resources to develop critical-thinking skills and are taught how to spot the stuff that's made up and that is designed specifically to mislead and create divisions in our society.

Earlier this year, I published my report *Growing Up Digital*, which set out the important role digital citizenship should be playing in schools. In the report, I wanted to broaden the conversation away from just 'internet safety' towards more active resilience-building in children. As part of that, we set out proposals for ensuring all children are educated about their digital rights in a way that chimes with their real-life experiences. Some of those digital citizenship lessons could focus on looking at what makes something fake news, and help children to develop skills encouraging them to analyse the news they read and hear, for example teaching them how to double-check facts against different sources and understand which sources are more likely to be trustworthy. It could also build resilience in children so they have the confidence to report and flag up fake news, helping to break the cycle of its distribution.

We also need to see more from the internet giants, who after all play such a big part in the lives of children. They have to take more responsibility for what children are reading on their sites and do more to stop fake news being circulated on their platforms. I support proposals for a social media levy to fund better protection of children, which could even include giving children better resources for learning to spot fake news, alongside greater transparency from the internet companies about how they deal with fake news on their own platforms.

If we want children to thrive and make the most of the brilliant innovations the digital world gives them, it is more important than ever that we make sure they have the information and the skills they need to make informed choices.

6 December 2017

Older children are getting wise to fake news

Older children are less trusting of news on social media than from other sources and use a range of measures to separate fact from fiction, Ofcom research has found.

More than half (54%) of 12- to 15-year-olds use social media platforms such as Facebook and Twitter, to access online news, making social media the second most popular source of news after television (62%).

The news children read through social media is provided by third-party websites. While some of these may be reputable news organisations, others may not.

But many children are wise to this. Just 32% of 12- to 15-year-olds who say social media is one of their top news sources believe news accessed through these sites is always, or mostly, reported truthfully, compared to 59% who say this about TV and 59% about radio.

Nearly three-quarters (73%) of online tweens are aware of the concept of "fake news", and four in ten (39%) say they have seen a fake news story online or on social media.

The findings are from Ofcom's *Children and Parents Media Use and Attitudes Report 2017*. This year, the report examines for the first time how children aged 12 to 15 consume news and online content.

Filtering fake news

The vast majority of 12–15s who follow news on social media are questioning the content they see. Almost nine in ten (86%) say they would make at least one practical attempt to check whether a social media news story is true or false.

The main approaches older children say they would take include:

⇨ **Seeing if the news story appears elsewhere** (48% of children who follow news on social media would do this).

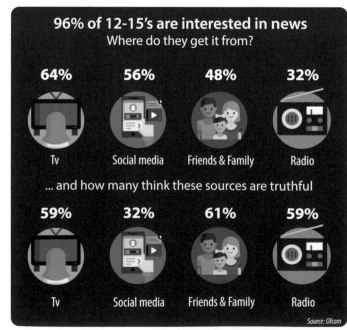

⇨ **Reading comments after the news report in a bid to verify its authenticity** (39%).

⇨ **Checking whether the organisation behind it is one they trust** (26%).

⇨ **Assessing the professional quality of the article** (20%).

Some 63% of 12- to 15-year-olds who are aware of fake news are prepared to do something about it, with 35% saying they would tell their parents or another family member; 18% would leave a comment saying they thought the news story was fake; and 14% would report the content to the social media website directly.

But some children still need help telling fact from fiction. Almost half (46%) of 12–15s who use social media for news say they find it difficult to tell whether a social media news story is true and 8% say they wouldn't make any checks.

Emily Keaney, Head of Children's Research at Ofcom, said: 'Most older children now use social media to access news, so it's vitally important they can take time to evaluate what they read, particularly as it isn't always easy to tell fact from fiction.

'It's reassuring that almost all children now say they have strategies for checking whether a social media news story is true or false. There may be two reasons behind this: lower trust in news shared through social media, but the digital generation are also becoming savvy online.'

29 November 2017

www.ofcom.org.uk

How to spot fake news

Reading, watching, and listening to the news is important for finding out what is going on in the world today. The majority of news we read is produced by companies we trust, but increasingly we have to be critical of the stories that we read. Some companies or individuals produce 'fake news' that is intended to mislead us, or make us change opinion.

But just how do we know that a story is false? Follow these tips to help you decide if what you are reading in the news is true or not.

Have you heard of the company before?
If you have, then the chances are that the story is real. Organisations such as Ofcom and the Independent Press Standards Organisation regulate press companies to ensure that they don't mislead people.

Can you find the same story elsewhere?
Check reputable news sites to see if you can find the same story. Sites such as the BBC, *The Independent, The Guardian, The Times, The Telegraph* etc. are good places to look.

Does the domain name look real?
Most sites should start with https:/ and end in either .com or .co.uk

Is it on social media?
If the source is reliable, such as from a reputable company, then it is more than likely true. However, if you don't recgonise the company, or it was posted by an individual, then it could be false.

Are there any statistics?
Is there a poll, or any facts and figures in the story? If they are real they will have a source that you will be able to check.

Do the facts check out?
If you are not sure about the facts and figures in the story then have a look at fullfact.org or snopes.com to see if you can find the truth.

Are there any links in the text?
Most articles contain links either in the text, or a list of references at the end of the article. By looking at the types of sources used, you will get a good idea that the story is trustworthy or not.

Does the story contain quotes?
If there are any quotes in the text from officials or experts, you will usually be able to find them quite easily by doing a search online.

Is it well-written?
If the spelling and grammar is poor, this could be an indication that the story is fake. Reputable sources use proof-readers and editors, and therefore would be less likely to contain mistakes.

Does the story seem provocative?
Most fake news stories spread quickly due to their ability to provoke a strong response in the reader. If it seems that the story is too provocative, or too good to be true, think twice before sharing it.

Why we age-rate films

Why do we do it?

All films shown in the UK need an age rating by law.

What are the ratings?

The BBFC rate films before they are released in cinemas. These days there are five certificates for cinema films

- **U**
- **PG**
- **12A**
- **15**
- **18**

In theory, anyone can see a U or a PG, although you and your parents and teachers are encouraged to think carefully about whether a PG film will be suitable for you if you are younger than eight years old.

With 12A films you must be 12 or older to go and see them, unless you have an adult with you. The accompanying adult must take responsibility for the younger child watching the film (and the BBFC recommends they read the ratings info for the film to help them decide whether it is likely to be suitable).

Anyone wanting to release a film, video or DVD for showing in cinemas or watching at home has to make sure that their film has a BBFC age rating symbol. It's against the law to try and sell videos and DVDs without this. Films that you see at the cinema also have to display the right rating.

When was the BBFC started?

The BBFC was created by the film industry in 1912, long before anyone had even heard of Harry Potter or Pixar. It wanted to make sure that all of its films, (videos and DVDs had not been invented then), were checked on behalf of the whole country. Cinemas needed a licence to show films because film stock burns very easily and there was a big fire risk.

Local councils, who were, and still are, in charge of cinemas up and down the country, grew to accept the BBFC's decisions. Even today, for films shown in cinemas, councils have the power to ignore any decision made by the BBFC and can give them their own age ratings. For example, in 1993, the comedy film *Mrs. Doubtfire* was given a 12 classification by the BBFC. Some councils disagreed with our decision and gave the film a PG.

An important change came with the arrival of video in the early 1980s. In 1984, a new law was passed, The Video Recordings Act, which put the BBFC in charge of classifying all videos for home use. The law asks Compliance Officers to make sure that works are classified for appropriate audiences and make sure that they show nothing that might be harmful to people, especially young children.

What does all this mean exactly?

Well, for example, very scary or gory horror films that might upset younger children are unlikely to be found at U, PG or 12A/12. As for harmful material, the BBFC has to note any dangerous or criminal activities on a video or DVD, such as scenes that show, in detail, how to hurt people or themselves and or scenes in which children are encouraged to do dangerous things, or take part in activities which could hurt them or those around them. Scenes like this may also be cut from the video before it's released to the public – though this is very rare.

The Compliance Officers at the BBFC also have to be aware of other laws, such as those which protect animals. It is against the law in this country to show films or videos in which an animal has been treated cruelly during the production. The owners of any film showing such a scene are asked to remove it (cut it out) before a certificate is given and the film is allowed to be released.

Filmmakers have always been allowed to get advice from the BBFC about the age rating their film will probably get. Sometimes they send in the film before it is finished, and Compliance Managers watch it without special effects, music or other details. The Compliance Managers can give a good idea of the rating the film will probably get based on our guidelines. If the filmmakers decide the likely rating is too high, they may decide to change the film, eg by removing scenes or changing the special effects, so they are more likely to get the lower rating they want. This is called a 'cut for category' and is the most common sort of cut made to films in the UK.

Now, as well as classifying films released in UK cinemas and on DVD and Blu-ray, the BBFC provide age-ratings for Video On Demand platforms.

www.bbfc.co.uk

British Board of Film Classification Age Ratings

 A U film should be suitable for audiences aged four years and over, although it is impossible to predict what might upset any particular child. U films should be set within a positive framework and should offer reassuring counterbalances to any violence, threat or horror.

A PG film should not unsettle a child aged around eight or older. Unaccompanied children of any age may watch, but parents are advised to consider whether the content may upset younger or more sensitive children.

 Films classified 12A and video works classified 12 contain material that is not generally suitable for children aged under 12.
No one younger than 12 may see a 12A film in a cinema unless accompanied by an adult. Adults planning to take a child under 12 to view a 12A film should consider whether the film is suitable for that child.
To help them decide, we recommend that they check the ratings info for that film in advance.
No one younger than 12 may rent or buy a 12 rated video work.

 No one younger than 15 may see a 15 film in a cinema.
No one younger than 15 may rent or buy a 15 rated video work.

No one younger than 18 may see an 18 film in a cinema.
No one younger than 18 may rent or buy an 18 rated video work.

Source: BBFC

Ghosts, liberated women and Morgan Freeman: the films banned for odd reasons

Wonder Woman *is the latest blockbuster to fall foul of the censors. From* Borat *to* Sex and the City 2, *here are some of the more peculiar film bans*

By Ben Child

The 'glory' days of the British censor – when grey-faced men would take a pair of scissors to every 1980's horror flick, from *Maniac* to *The Evil Dead*, while the tabloids screamed 'video nasty' in the background – are thankfully gone. These days it takes something truly horrific – a *Human Centipede 2* or a *Hate Crime* – to ruffle the feathers of the British Board of Film Classification (BBFC). Not to worry, for the grand tradition of banning movies remains firmly extant in other corners of the world. This week Lebanon refused to grant the comic book-action flick *Wonder Woman* a theatrical release on the grounds that its star is from Israel, at a time when the two countries are at war. While the merits of the ban have been hotly debated online, what is clear is that it's not the only film to fall foul of the censors in recent years. Here are some of the more unlikely of those film bans:

The Uzbek thriller banned for not starring Morgan Freeman

If you've been to the cinema much over the past decade or so, you might be under the impression that Morgan Freeman is in every film. If a Hollywood producer is looking for a senior alpha male, primed to deliver lines of grandiloquent yet pithy wisdom at just the right moment, Freeman is most definitely their man. But just because it seems as if the *Shawshank Redemption* star is ubiquitous on the big screen, that doesn't mean it's OK to pretend he's in your film when he's not – as the Uzbekistan production studio Timur Film discovered in February. Posters for the action thriller *Daydi* (*Rogue*) featured a hooded Freeman between two local actors. Unfortunately, this was the Hollywood star's one and only contribution to the movie, as he does not appear in a single frame of the film. *Daydi* was duly banned by Uzbekistan's film licensing body, which we like to imagine being staffed almost entirely by outraged fans of *Driving Miss Daisy*.

When Borat *was banned for upsetting* Kazakhstan

Sacha Baron Cohen's 2006 comedy depicts its dubious hero's homeland as a place where racists and criminals are on every run-down street corner, but (in Borat's own words) the 'prostitutes are the cleanest in the region'. Not surprisingly, authorities in Kazakhstan did not take too kindly to its rendering, and prohibited the movie from release in cinemas. *Borat* was also banned by Russia and every Arab country except Lebanon, with a censor at Dubai's ministry of information labelling the comedy 'vile, gross and extremely ridiculous', adding that if all the offensive scenes were cut out, only 30 minutes would remain. Attitudes towards the movie in Kazakhstan do appear to have shifted, however: *Borat* was a huge hit when released on DVD in 2007, and in 2012 the nation's foreign minister, Yerzhan Kazykhanov, thanked the films makers for helping to increase tourism to the country. 'With the release of this film, the number of visas issued by Kazakhstan grew tenfold,' he said.

Sex and the City 2 *banned in the UAE for showing liberated women*

There are many honest cinema goers who wish *Sex and the City 2* had been outlawed worldwide. But the decision by United Arab Emirates censors to ban the critically reviled comedy sequel, in which Carrie Bradshaw and her New York gal pals head to Abu Dhabi on holiday, still makes uncomfortable reading. Officials were unhappy at scenes referencing homosexuality and highly displeased by a sequence in which one of the main characters is shown kissing in public, according to local reports. The most galling scene, however, appears to have been one in which the four ladies are rescued by Muslim women – who take off their burqas to reveal stylish western clothes underneath.

Ghostbusters *banned in China for promoting superstition*

No one can say Sony didn't do its best to secure a Chinese release for the all-female remake of the classic 80's comedy last year. Executives even proposed renaming the movie Super Power Dare-to-Die Team in order to try and avoid upsetting local censors. But it would be hard to come away from watching *Ghostbusters* without being at least partly aware that the movie is about... well, ghosts. And ghosts are a taboo subject in the world's most populous nation, due to communist views on the supernatural: official Chinese censorship guidance prohibit films that 'promote cults or superstition'. A source told the *Hollywood Reporter* in July last year that Paul Feig's film would not be getting a release, but refused to confirm this was due to the movie's spooky subject matter.

That time the Philippines banned every Claire Danes movie

Woe betide the Hollywood star who slags off shooting conditions in a foreign country during a routine magazine interview, then discovers that, thanks to the internet, it isn't just Americans who can access *Vogue*'s website. This is what happened to the *Homeland* star, who described the Philippines capital, Manila, as 'a ghastly and weird city' during the promotion for her 1999 drug mule drama *Brokedown Palace*, then compounded the issue by telling *Premiere* the metropolis 'smelled of cockroaches, with rats all over, [had] no sewerage system,' and was populated by people with 'no arms, no legs, no eyes'. Then-president Joseph Estrada, himself a former movie star, called for Danes to be banned from the country, and Manila's city council banned every film starring the *Romeo + Juliet* actor from screening in cinemas there. Danes later issued an apology, saying that 'because of the subject matter of our film *Brokedown Palace*, the cast was exposed to the darker and more impoverished places of Manila'. But local politicians were unimpressed and refused to lift the ban – which as far as we can tell, remains in place.

When North Korea banned 2012 *for failing to stick to the script*

Roland Emmerich's apocalyptic 2009 disaster flick features a global geological catastrophe that almost wipes out the human race. This did not go down well with the leadership of the rogue nation, for whom the year 2012 has significance, not for being the date on which the Mayans predicted the end of the world, but for supposedly marking the beginning of North Korea's rise to the status of global superpower. This prediction was based on 2012 being the 100th anniversary of the birth of Kim Il-Sung, founder of the nation, and North Koreans who illegally purchased DVDs from China were punished with up to five years in prison for watching a movie that dared to suggest history might turn out differently. The irony is that *2012*, with its depiction of American cities such as Los Angeles sinking into the Pacific, would probably have proven quite cheery viewing for the North Korean high command.

2 June 2017

Why does China's Xi hate Winnie the Pooh?

By Cindy Yu

Why is Winnie the Pooh like Ai Weiwei? Both have landed in political hot water with the Chinese government. The artist Ai has a long history of running into trouble with the Chinese authorities. In fact, earlier this week, Ai's Beijing studio was demolished for reasons unknown (though perhaps you can take a guess). And Pooh's become an equally worthy dissident, all because he bears an unfortunate resemblance to President Xi Jinping. Judging by his waistline, President Xi is obviously settling in to his cushy job with too much tea and honey. And he's feeling sensitive about it. So much so that Disney's upcoming film about Pooh bear, *Christopher Robin*, has been banned in China.

How did the world's most successful authoritarian regime get so touchy about a cartoon bear? It all started in 2013, when Xi met Obama. The picture that came out of the meeting shows the two men walking side-by-side – one of the better diplomatic pictures to have come out of world leader meetings, you might think. That was until someone, rather astutely, posted the pic next to a picture of Pooh walking with the rather taller, thinner Tigger. The resemblance was – and is – quite amusing, but I'm not sure Beijing is known for its humour.

Censors quickly took down the image. And just as any common sense could have told you, this repression made the easygoing tongue-in-cheek comparison into an irresistible big red button. Cue Chinese 'netizens' conducting experiments on social media to see if their Pooh

will be deleted. Some of them were, some of them weren't. But even if the censorship wasn't a blanket ban, the harm had been done. A.A. Milne's loveable bear had now been turned into a fully-fledged symbol of sarcastic resistance in the meme age.

Perhaps President Xi and his gaggle of censors can learn from Milne. As Christopher Robin says to Pooh: 'you're braver than you believe'. As leader of the world's rising power, it's time Xi learned to brush off these small trivial acts of rebellion.

8 August 2018

Mary Whitehouse was right: why, even in the streaming age, we need the watershed more than ever

By Michael Hogan

Watch with mother? Not any more. Already this century, many developments have transformed the way we watch TV: bingeing on boxsets; the rise of streaming and catch-up services; the ability to watch programmes not just on that big box in the corner of the sitting room but on laptops, tablets, mobile phones and, no doubt soon, the inside of one's eyelids.

Many now believe that modern technology has rendered the 9pm watershed meaningless and is making a mockery of TV's increasingly redundant ratings system. So is the TV watershed about to experience, well, a watershed moment?

Thanks to on-demand, catch-up and multiple screens in homes, we now have 12-year-olds watching the likes of *Game Of Thrones* (dragons and bare flesh) and *Love Island* (dimwits and bare flesh), whenever they want, often without their parents even knowing.

A recent survey of GoT viewer demographics found that 8.2% are under-18s and psychologists have expressed concerns about their exposure to the HBO epic's regular scenes of sexual violence.

The percentage for *Love Island* is thought to be much higher, with many watching through the ITV Hub on-demand platform – probably away from prying parental eyes. Public health charities have already warned that the reality flirt-fest is seducing teens into smoking. It could be encouraging them to "gaslight" and "slut-shame" too.

In days of yore, sulky teenagers would announce they were 'going upstairs to play my tapes' (copyright Tracy Barlow on *Coronation Street*), before stomping up to their bedroom and slamming the door shut. The modern equivalents are gaming, Whatsapping or Snapchatting their mates – and watching *The Walking Dead, Riverdale* or RuPaul's *Drag Race* on their iPads.

Stats show that two-thirds of 11-to-15-year-olds use smartphones and most of them watch video online. Teenagers also consume one-third less broadcast TV on traditional sets than they did in 2010. When the biggest

barrier is a 'yes, I'm over 16' tickbox (hardly fibber-proof), preventing children from watching inappropriate material is increasingly a challenge.

Perhaps this isn't surprising, since the watershed was designed for a very different era, more than half a century ago. Introduced in 1964 under pressure from pearl-clutching conservative crusader Mary Whitehouse and her Clean Up TV campaign, it's a relic of a time long before Netflix and YouTube were even a twinkle in Tim Berners-Lee's eye.

Broadly speaking, we all know what the watershed means: no explicit sex, graphic violence, strong language or distressing images before 9pm, with the aim of protecting children. (It's less well-known that the watershed ends at 5.30am the following morning, but unless reruns of *Flog It!* take a dark turn, that's academic.)

Thus 9pm has long been established as the pivotal point of the evening's TV – the witching hour, the send-them-to-bed reminder, the dividing line between family-friendly shows and those aimed at a more adult audience.

However, 21st - century TV is a moveable feast. Regardless of what time they're aired, post-watershed shows get downloaded and streamed at all times of the day by viewers well under the age of 18. Or 16. Or even 12. The watershed worked best when there was a single TV in the family home. It's nowhere near as effective now there are multiple screens, both around the house and on the move, and technology has liberated viewing from the what's-on-when linear schedules.

For a start, regulation of streaming services is fiendishly complicated. Ofcom can enforce standards and levy fines at Amazon Prime Video, while Netflix falls within the jurisdiction of Holland, so has to abide by EU directives and the Dutch regulator. Clear as mud? Thought so.

This grey area came into stark focus last year when high school saga *13 Reasons Why* landed on Netflix. Its graphic depictions of suicide, self-harm and rape prompted concerns from mental health and education professionals.

The Samaritans said it could trigger troubled young people into copycat behaviour. Studies showed a 26 per cent spike in suicide-related web searches. New Zealand banned under-18s from watching it without an adult. Two Austrian schoolgirls are believed to have attempted to kill themselves after watching the series.

For the first time, parents began to realise just how lawless streaming services are. They had no idea their kids were watching a show rated for over-15s or over-18s, depending on which country you're in, let alone one so potentially harmful. London-based child psychologist Dr Nicole Gehl said that she found the first series 'really disturbing', having 'started watching after I had 11-year-old patients talking about it'.

In response, Netflix added pre-credits warnings and followed episodes with details of mental health resources. However, it was worrying that it took widespread criticism to achieve this. Despite calls from parent groups for 13 Reasons Why to be pulled, Netflix has just renewed it for a third series.

All this is why "media futurologists" – what a insufferable term that is - have been forecasting the demise of the 9pm watershed for some time. Indeed, in 2015, BBC director-general Tony Hall said: "Has the watershed got a future in 20 or 30 years' time? I suspect not." And if you can't trust a 67-year-old baron's predictions about technology, what can you trust?

Despite the doom-mongering, though, it doesn't look like the watershed is going to disappear any time soon – and especially under a Conservative government. Rightly so, because it still plays an important part in the protection of our children and maintaining public confidence in TV during this fractured era.

Statistics back this up. Ofcom research shows that 93 per cent of viewers understand what the watershed is and 74 per cent think 9pm is the right time for it. When just parents are asked, that number creeps up to 76%. The regulator takes action most weeks against broadcasters who break the rules, finding over 400 programmes which breached its

guidelines in the last decade – the most notorious recent example being an overly sexualised S&M routine from Rihanna on the pre-watershed X Factor. The watchdog's teeth might not be as sharp as Whitehouse would have liked, but Ofcom still bares them.

Then there's the gap between the media bubble perception of people's viewing habits and the reality. The future of TV hasn't arrived as fast as many pundits would have you believe. In spite of the explosion of choice and tech, more of us are watching more hours of linear TV than ever before, averaging four hours per day.

Big communal shows – be it Bake Off or Love Island, the World Cup or Royal Wedding – still lend themselves to live viewing and "second screening" on social networks as the action unfolds. However unfashionable it may seem among millennials, the TV schedule is very much alive and kicking.

So it seems rumours of the watershed's death have been greatly exaggerated. As content proliferates and social standards evolve, a widely agreed barometer of taste is more useful than ever. The watershed is a rule of thumb still clearly understood by viewers, helping them navigate the now-sprawling TV landscape. It gives a handy steer about what to expect from a show (at 7.30pm, you're probably fine but by 9pm, exercise caution) and prevents scheduling anarchy.

The watershed may not cure all cultural ills but along with technological safeguards – PIN codes, parental locks, WiFi curfews, hard drive checks – it's a valuable tool to help reassure parents and protect children. And frankly, any kind of guidance in these confusing times can only be a good thing. I never thought I'd hear myself say it but well done, Mary Whitehouse.

28 June 2018

Snowflakes and trigger warnings: Shakespearean violence has always upset people

THE CONVERSATION

An article from The Conversation.

By Rebecca Yearling, Lecturer in English, Keele University

We are repeatedly told that today's young people are oversensitive, claiming to need "trigger warnings" and to be traumatised by literary texts – including the works of Shakespeare – that previous generations took in their stride. But is it really true that readers and theatre-goers of the past were more emotionally resilient than today's "snowflake" generation?

In his 1765 edition of *The Plays of William Shakespeare*, the great 18th-century critic Samuel Johnson admitted that reading certain scenes in Shakespeare's *King Lear* gave him a sense of extreme discomfort. He found the death of Lear's daughter, Cordelia, in the tragedy's last act, so upsetting that he avoided ever reading the scene again until he was forced to do so by his work as an editor.

Moreover, he claimed, the blinding of the elderly Gloucester in the middle of the play was so terrible that a theatre spectator would not be able to cope with it. He described it as an act 'too horrid to be endured in dramatic exhibition'.

Was Johnson a snowflake, too? If he was, then so were many others of his time. There is a long history of censoring and rewriting the plays of Shakespeare in order to make them less traumatic to their readers and spectators.

Censoring Shakespeare's violence

In 1681, *King Lear* was rewritten by the dramatist Nahum Tate with a revised, happy ending in which both Cordelia and her father live – and this was so popular with audiences that Tate's adaptation was the only version of the play to be performed on stage for the next 150 years.

Meanwhile, another notably violent Shakespeare play, *Titus Andronicus*, was similarly rewritten. *Titus* features a female character who is raped, and subsequently has her tongue cut out and her hands cut off to prevent her from telling the names of her attackers. When the play appeared onstage in England in 1850, all this material was removed.

As a contemporary reviewer wrote: 'The deflowerment of Lavinia, cutting out her tongue, chopping off her hands... are wholly omitted'. As the reviewer went on to comment, the play then seemed 'not only presentable but actually attractive as a result'.

The violence was not the only thing that readers and spectators found upsetting about Shakespeare's plays. Race and sexuality also caused problems. The US president John Quincy Adams wrote in 1786 that although he thought *Othello* in many respects a great work, he found the mixed-race relationship at its heart, 'injudicious, disgusting, and contrary to all probability'.

Other prominent figures also expressed their reservations about aspects of Shakespeare. Queen Victoria, for example, criticised the plays for their sexual humour. She wrote to her eldest daughter in 1859 that she had never 'had the courage' to see Shakespeare's *Merry Wives of Windsor* on stage, 'having always been told how very coarse it was – for your adored Shakespeare is dreadful in that respect, and many things have to be left out in many plays'.

Censoring the plays in print

To counter these and similar objections, a market developed for censored print editions of the plays. In 1815, Thomas and Harriet Bowdler published The Family Shakespeare in order 'to present to the public an edition of his Plays, which the parent, the guardian, and the instructor of youth, may place without fear in the hands of the pupil'.

The Bowdlers edited 20 of Shakespeare's plays for this publication, removing swear words and many of the references to sex and violence. They also changed plots to make them less potentially distressing – the death of Ophelia in *Hamlet*, for example, became an accidental drowning, to avoid disturbing readers with a portrayal of an apparent suicide.

The Bowdlers were criticised by some of their contemporaries for having gone too far in tampering with these classic works – but their edition was still hugely popular and, by the end of the 19th century, hundreds more censored versions of Shakespeare's plays had appeared in print.

A disturbing playwright

Race, violence, sexuality, suicide: many of the things that modern students have been accused of finding upsetting about the plays are exactly what bothered readers and spectators of the past. Shakespeare has never been a safe or reassuring playwright and his works have always been capable of disturbing their audiences.

The specifics of what is found offensive may alter, of course: most modern critics of *Othello* have been more concerned about whether the depiction of the title character is itself racist than worried about whether the play advocates for mixed-race marriage.

Nevertheless, we should rethink the idea that there is something uniquely or unusually fragile about today's young people in their response to Shakespeare, when such a claim is contradicted by the evidence of the past.

22 November 2018

www.theconversation.com

Should books ever be banned?

Back in 1925, Adolf Hitler wrote a book called *Mein Kampf* which shared his thoughts and plans for running Germany. Essentially, it was an outpouring of hatred, detailing the principles that later guided his Nazi regime. A system that – we now know from history – caused the deaths and torture of millions of people.

But should this book be banned today? Could it inspire other people to repeat history? This is a tricky area and one that Germany has had to deal with only very recently. At the end of World War Two, it was decided that no new publications of the book could be made. But the problem was there were already 70 million copies printed and in circulation, and it wasn't illegal to own one. In 2012, the German government had to start thinking about what they could do when the book's copyright expired at the end of 2015 – meaning that it could now be published freely again. In the end, they decided to publish a new, scholarly, annotated version of the text. In other words, the book would include explanations by experts on the meanings of key words and phrases. There would also be information about the book's history and its social impact on people living in Austria at the time it was written and beyond. This way, it was hoped that the book would be educational for its readers.

Sebastian Huempfer thinks this is a good idea. He says that banning a book gives it a sense of power and glamour.

'If you read [*Mein Kampf*], it's a garbled mess of nonsense,' he points out. 'If you tell people it's dangerous [and] you're not going to let anyone read it, that makes it sound like it's powerful and seductive [attractive] in a way that it really isn't.'

What about in school?

But it's not just about what a government might say or do. Books might be banned by a school if the staff think they're inappropriate for students to read – or an individual teacher might decide not to teach a particular book because of its content.

This still happens today. Judy Blume's books for teenagers have been taken out of some school libraries around the world for their frank discussion of sex, and Philip Pullman's *His Dark Materials* trilogy was banned in some American schools for the way it wrote about religion. Even Roald Dahl's *Revolting Rhymes* has shocked some parents and teachers because of some of the gruesome ways his fairy-tale characters die!

Huempfer says there are plenty of reasons why a book may be banned in a school. Teachers might decide a book is inappropriate for their classes, or librarians may not purchase a book for the library; even the Harry Potter series has been banned in some schools for its spooky and magical storylines. He also points out that sometimes school staff are worried about bringing up difficult topics – such as sex, religion, racism or death – and so they avoid books that talk about them, even if they don't ban them completely.

Taking a platform

The arguments around banning books are reflected in real-life as students and universities tackle the idea of 'no-platforming'. This means when certain people are refused from speaking at events because their views are so outrageous and/or offensive. This happened at Manchester University in 2016 when feminist writer, Julie Bindel was stopped from speaking at the students' union due to her controversial opinions on transgender people.

'Students who are in favour of no-platforming would argue that it's a type of self-expression. It's a way for the University to say, "This is the kind of university we want to be and we don't want to give certain people a platform".' says Huempfer.

But – he says that – historically if you believe in free speech, you also believe in showing why you disagree with people by putting forward your arguments – not by stopping your opponents from speaking.

Huempfer thinks the current generation of young people understand the value of all kinds of freedom of speech much more than their parents or grandparents. With so many ways in which to express your opinions – from social media to online comments to political activism – he says that young people really appreciate their opportunities to be heard.

'It's a moment when there are a much greater variety of voices and a much smaller trust in authority,' he says. Protests such as the March for Europe and the development of smaller political parties such as the Women's Equality Party are good examples of this.

Freedom of speech is really important – but what if people want to say or write something really offensive? Should everyone be able to say exactly what they like? This is a big debate that isn't going away any time soon – instead, it's time for you to make up your mind.

www.oxplore.org

How censorship through the decades cracked down on literary sex, drugs... and poo poo head

It's Banned Books Week, and this year the UK is taking a bigger role in fighting censorship, writes David Barnett.

Consider suppressed books and what do you think of? Someone carefully measuring out the ingredients for a bomb in their mother's cellar, poring over *The Anarchist's Cookbook*? A 1980's Britain supposedly blissfully unaware of the revelations in Peter Wright's banned MI5 memoir *Spycatcher*, while the rest of the world laps up his allegations? Well-thumbed copies of *Lady Chatterley's Lover* being passed surreptitiously between filth-hungry readers?

Or do you perhaps think of the Great Poo Poo Head Incident of 2011?

Allow me to remind you of that one. Back then, Tammy and Randy Harris's son was six years old. He was given a one-day suspension from his school in Texas for deploying with wild abandon the phrase 'poo poo head'.

Which might seem a bit harsh. But then Tammy discovered that the self-same epithet uttered by her son was also to be found in a book kept in the school library, to wit *The Adventures of Super Diaper Baby*, a graphic novel from the same creators behind the hugely popular Captain Underpants series of prose books.

Was it fair that her son was sent home from school for saying 'poo poo head' when those exact words were in a book on the school library shelf? So Tammy Harris demanded that the book be removed from the school.

Her demand was rejected at first, but following an appeal and a fresh investigation into the incident, an education committee upheld her complaint and *The Adventures of Super Diaper Baby* was duly banned from that Texas school.

So when we talk about book bannings, we're not necessarily discussing Nazi-style bonfires of books... though that still happens. A couple of years ago ISIS torched Mosul library and everything in it. But what is more common are incidents such as the Poo Poo Head one, in which parents take exception to something found in a book their child has procured from school, and immediately try to get it withdrawn from circulation.

It happens a lot in America, of course, and that is why Banned Books Week, which begins on 24 September, has been an annual event since 1982. A loose coalition of anti-censorship organisations band together for the awareness-raising event, and each year the American Library Association releases a list of the 'most challenged' books across the States.

By far the biggest reason given for complaining about books is that they have characters who are lesbian, gay, transgender or bisexual, or stories which deal with these themes. And the complaints are not because LGBT characters or issues are dealt with poorly; it's because they're there at all.

The most-complained about book in 2016 was *This One Summer*, a graphic novel written by Mark Tamaki and illustrated by her cousin Jillian Tamaki. It's a coming-of-age story that was frequently challenged, according to the ALA, because of its 'LGBT characters, drug use and profanity, and it was considered sexually explicit with mature themes'.

Alex Gino's 2015 novel *George*, which features a transgender lead character, was wanted off the shelves because 'sexuality was not appropriate at elementary levels', while *The Fault In Our Stars* author John Green's *Looking For Alaska* was challenged for a sexually explicit scene that may lead a student to 'sexual experimentation'.

It isn't all redneck outrage against non-heterosexual relationships of course, though it mainly is. In the top ten of last year's most complained about books was the *Little Bill* series written by Bill Cosby, by dint of the high-profile sexual assault allegations surrounding him.

Banned Books Week takes a Voltairean stance on book bannings; you don't have to like what's in the book to disagree with censorship. In 2015 someone wanted E.L. James *50 Shades of Grey* banned because it was 'poorly written'; well, a lot of people might think that, but it's not really a reason for it to be suppressed, nor is the fact that it's full of kinky sex. The good thing about books is that if what's inside them is deemed offensive, you can't see it until you open the covers.

We might expect that book bannings are a particularly American thing, but this year Banned Books Week is a bigger thing in the UK than it ever has been before, largely due to the involvement of the non-profit campaign Index for Censorship.

'Censorship isn't something that happens far away,' says Jodie Ginsberg, the campaign's CEO. 'It has happened in the UK. In every library there are books that British citizens have been blocked from reading at various times. As citizens and literature lovers we must be constantly vigilant to guard against the erosion of our freedom to read.

'Index is excited to be joining the coalition as the first non-US member. We have been publishing work by censored writers from around the world for 45 years and – given all that is happening on the global political stage – it feels more important than ever to be highlighting censorship and demonstrating just what it means when books are banned.'

Charles Brownsein, chair of the Banned Books Week Coalition and executive director of the Comic Book Legal Defence Fund, which finances comic book creators and retailers court cases against censorship actions, is delighted that the primarily US event now has a foothold in the UK. He says, 'We are very excited to have the Index on Censorship join the coalition. Their work not only aligns with our mission, but will bring an international perspective and awareness to our annual celebration of the freedom to read.'

There are a series of events taking place this coming week, many of them at the British Library in London, including on Tuesday a talk by Katherine Inglis and Matthew Fellion, authors of a new book on suppressed literature; an investigation into the Salman Rushdie *Satanic Verses* affair which saw the author go into hiding as his book was burned in Bradford (Thursday) and on Saturday 30 September a look at the controversial novel by J.G. Ballard, *Crash*, with Will Self and Chris Beckett, followed by a screening of David Cronenberg's movie adaptation.

The events show the breadth of work that has been banned, suppressed or called for removal from shops, libraries and schools. According to Lisa Appignanesi, chair of the Royal Society of Literature, 'It's an irony that the list of books banned over the last centuries, whether by religious or political authorities jealous of their power, constitutes the very best of our literatures.

'From the Bible to Thomas Paine, Flaubert, G.B. Shaw to Simone de Beauvoir's *The Second Sex* and Rushdie's *The Satanic Verses*, some of the greatest of our books have been banned somewhere. Luckily humans have a way of valuing the prohibited and cherishing liberty; and this as George Orwell reminded us, "means the right to tell people what they do not want to hear".'

So if you're going to celebrate Banned Books Week, what should you be reading to show your support? Penguin Books has put together a handy list of the books they tried to ban (and in some cases did), and some of them might seem surprising.

Lady Chatterley's Lover by D.H. Lawrence we've already mentioned, and its publication in 1960 led to one of the most famous obscenity law trials in history. But what about George Orwell's *Animal Farm*, banned in the Soviet Republic in the 1980s because of its portrayal of a brutal dictatorship. Well, if the cap fits… And then there's Geoffrey Chaucer's *Canterbury Tales*, the earthy wit and saucy humour of which found it out of favour in 19th-century America.

Pretty much any Roald Dahl book has come under the censors' spotlights at some point, especially in the States. *The BFG* was once accused of 'promoting cannabilsm', but it's *The Witches* that has proven especially notorious, with complaints levelled at it including that it contains Satanic themes, turns children towards the occult, and doesn't do a very good job of upholding moral values.

Or maybe you could just track down a copy of George Beard and Harold Hutchins' *The Adventures of Super Diaper Baby*, and spend the week shouting 'poo poo head' at the top of your voice.

Because as anyone knows, and as Texan parents Tammy and Randy Harris learned swiftly, the moment you call for something to be banned, interest in it rockets. Back in the 1980s, more people were determined to get their hands on *Spycatcher* than ever bothered reading it just because they'd been told by the British government they weren't allowed to have it.

As Randy Harris said, appearing somewhat mystified, when the couple were interviewed by US TV channel ABC13 on their successful bid to get Diaper Baby cleared from the school shelves, 'Every kid in that school knows about that book. And every kid wants to check that book out.'

22 September 2017

www.independent.co.uk

What do protests about Harry Potter books teach us?

THE CONVERSATION

An article from The Conversation.

By Trisha Tucker, Assistant Professor of Writing, University of Southern California – Dornsife College of Letters, Arts and Sciences

On Monday, 26th June 2017, Harry James Potter – the world's most famous wizard – will celebrate his 20th birthday. His many fans will likely mark the occasion by rereading a favourite Harry Potter novel or rewatching one of the blockbuster films. Some may even raise a butterbeer toast in Harry's honour at one of three Harry Potter-themed amusement parks.

But not everyone will be celebrating Harry's big day. In fact, a vocal group of Christians – usually identified as "Bible-believing" or fundamentalist Christians – has been resistant to Harry's charms from the start. Members of this community, who believe the Bible to be literal truth, campaigned vigorously to keep J.K. Rowling's best-selling novels out of classrooms and libraries. They even staged public book burnings across the country, at which children and parents were invited to cast Rowling's books into the flames. These fiery spectacles garnered widespread media coverage, sparking reactions ranging from bemusement to outrage.

What could justify the use of such drastic measures to keep these books out of the hands of young readers?

The different views on Harry Potter

Book burnings may be relatively rare in modern America, but efforts to protect young readers from "dangerous" texts are not. Such texts, and the efforts to limit their readership, are the subject of a class I teach at the University of Southern California.

In this class, students survey a collection of books that have been challenged on moral, political and religious grounds. These include classics such as *1984* and *To Kill a Mockingbird,* as well as newer texts like *Persepolis* and *The Perks of Being a Wallflower.* The point is not to determine which challenges are "good" and which are "bad". Instead, we seek to understand how differing beliefs about reading and subjectivity make certain texts seem dangerous and others seem safe to particular populations of readers.

Harry Potter is one of the first books we discuss.

Most readers of Rowling's novel – including many Christian readers – interpret the characters' tutelage in spells and potions as harmless fantasy, or as metaphors for the development of wisdom and knowledge. Similarly, they read incidents in which Harry and his friends disobey adults or make questionable choices as opportunities for characters and readers alike to learn important lessons and begin to develop their own moral and ethical codes.

For some fundamentalist Christians, however, Harry's magical exploits pose an active danger. According to them, Hogwarts teaches the kinds of witchcraft explicitly condemned as punishable by death and damnation in the biblical books of Deuteronomy and Exodus. They believe the books must be banned – even burned – because their positive portrayal of magic is likely to attract unsuspecting children to real-world witchcraft.

Similarly, they think that when Harry disobeys his cruel Muggle guardians or flouts Dumbledore's rules to save his friends, he actively encourages child readers to engage in lying and disobedience, which are explicitly forbidden by the Bible. As Evangelical writer Richard Abanes puts it,

'The morals and ethics in Rowling's fantasy tales are at best unclear, and at worst, patently unbiblical.'

Making assumptions

Why don't Bible-believing Christians trust young readers to discern the difference between fantasy and reality? And why don't they think children can learn positive lessons from Harry's adventures – like the importance of standing up to injustice?

According to scholar Christine Jenkins, people who try to censor texts often hold a set of false assumptions about how reading works.

One of those assumptions is that particular literary content (like positive portrayals of witchcraft) will invariably produce particular effects (more witches in real life). Another is that reactions to a particular text are likely to be consistent across readers. In other words, if one reader finds a passage scary, funny or offensive, the assumption is that other readers invariably will do so as well.

As Jenkins points out, however, research has shown that readers' responses are highly variable and contextual. In fact, psychologists Amie Senland and Elizabeth Vozzola have demonstrated this about readers of Harry Potter.

In their study comparing the perceptions of fundamentalist and liberal Christian readers of Harry Potter, Senland and Vozzola reveal that different reading responses are possible in even relatively homogeneous groups. On the one hand, despite adults' fears to the contrary, few children in either group believed that the magic practiced in Harry Potter could be replicated in real life. On the other, the children disagreed about a number of things, including whether or not Dumbledore's bending of the rules for Harry made Dumbledore harder to respect.

Senland and Vozzola's study joins a body of scholarship that indicates that children perform complex negotiations as they read. Children's reading experiences are informed by both their unique personal histories and their cultural contexts.

In other words, there's no "normal" way to read Harry Potter – or any other book, for that matter.

Distrusting child readers

Fundamentalist Christians aren't the only group who have trouble trusting the capabilities of child readers.

Take the case of *To Kill a Mockingbird*.

For decades, parents have argued that Harper Lee's novel poses a danger to young readers, and have sought to remove it from classrooms for this reason. Some parents worry that the novel's vulgar language and sexual content will corrupt children's morals, while others fear that the novel's marginalisation of black characters will damage the self-image of black readers.

Despite their different ideological orientations, I believe that both of these groups of protesters – like the fundamentalists who attempt to censor Harry Potter – are driven by surprisingly similar misapprehensions about reading.

In all of these cases, the protesters presume that being exposed to a phenomenon in literature (whether witchcraft, foul language or racism) naturally leads to a reproduction of that phenomenon in life. They also believe that their individual experience of a text is correct and applicable to disparate readers.

These cases of attempted censorship show a profound distrust of child readers and their imaginations. And they ignore evidence that child readers are far more sophisticated than adults tend to credit them for.

26 June 2017

The State of Artistic freedom 2018

The emergence of a new global culture of silencing others.
An extract from the report **The State of Artistic Freedom 2018.**

In a world full of noise and information, many are silenced. Individuals and artists around the world find themselves voiceless, despite information and communication technology, and social media that allow people to express themselves and share their experiences and points of view.

Women in Iran are not allowed to perform solo singing, while women in Saudi Arabia are not allowed to sing in front of men. Thousands of artists from ethnic minorities are subjected to persecution and threats for singing and performing their arts in their own languages. Oromo artists in Ethiopia are prosecuted on terrorism charges. Rappers in Spain are sentenced under anti-terror legislation. Concert-goers in the UK faced a bombing, while others in Egypt were arrested and sentenced to two years in prison for waving a rainbow flag in support of LGBT artists. In Uzbekistan, 225 films were banned in one blacklist in 2017, while 130 books faced the same fate in Algeria.

On average, at least one artist was prosecuted per week in 2017. Together, they were sentenced to over 188 years in prison this year alone. Forty-eight artists were serving terms in prison for exercising their rights and expressing their views and feelings. Thousands of artists and artworks were banned. Freedom of artistic expression and creativity is being attacked at every front in every region of the world. In this process, a new global culture is emerging, one where censorship, attacks, prosecutions and other practices of silencing views one disagrees with is becoming the norm, driven both by governments and supported by large groups of people in society. This report documents and examines 553 cases of violations of artistic freedom in 78 countries carried out in 2017. It exposes violators and assesses the patterns and contexts of these violations. This research identifies groups of artists and people who are vulnerable to violations, especially women, minorities and LGBT people. It asks why, with such a large scale of attacks and abuses of artists around the world, there is little accountability.

The global culture of silencing others

2017 was the year of a new rise of popular nationalist politics in the US and Eastern Europe, built on Brexit, the Trump election and nationalist rhetoric in Poland and Hungary in the previous year. Populist politics won elections through words of fear and hatred of foreigners. This vision of society without immigrants, refugees and "others" gave nationalist politicians the votes they needed at the cost of dividing society. The rhetoric of hate and attacking messages from populist-nationalist leaders over a period of time creates legitimacy in dismissing "others" who are different, resulting in wide intolerance. This has created an enabling environment for large-scale and systematic violations of freedom of artistic expression as we have witnessed in 2017.

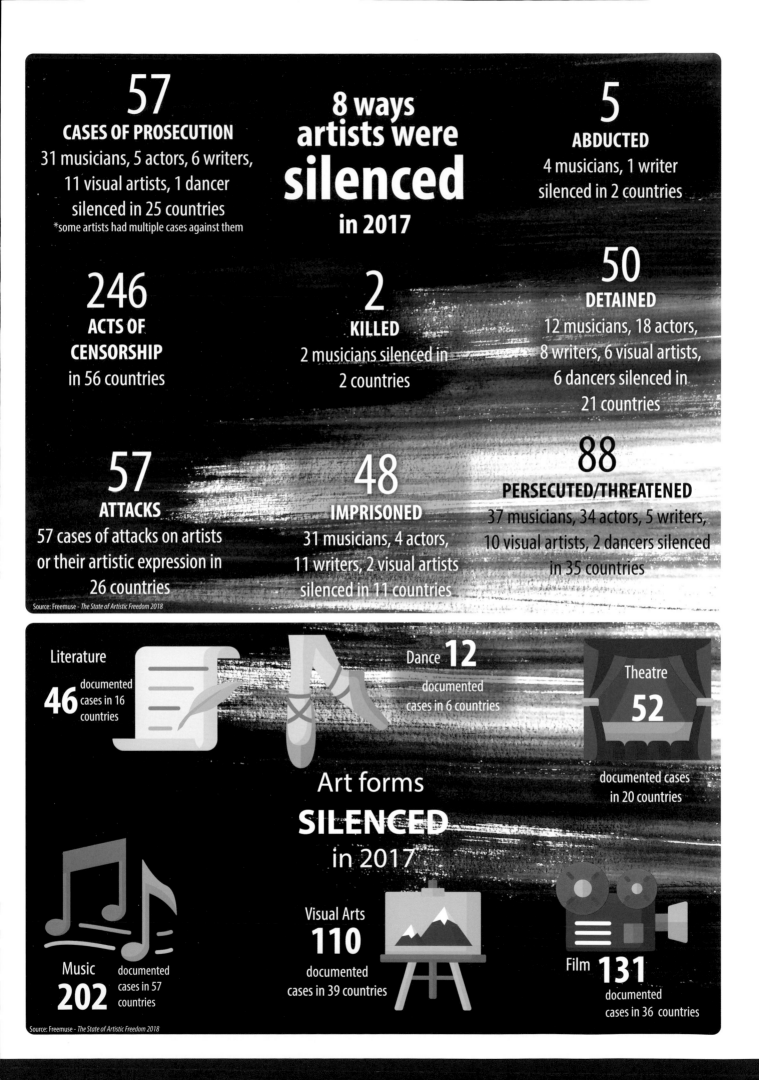

57
CASES OF PROSECUTION
31 musicians, 5 actors, 6 writers,
11 visual artists, 1 dancer
silenced in 25 countries
*some artists had multiple cases against them

**8 ways
artists were
silenced
in 2017**

5
ABDUCTED
4 musicians, 1 writer
silenced in 2 countries

246
**ACTS OF
CENSORSHIP**
in 56 countries

2
KILLED
2 musicians silenced in
2 countries

50
DETAINED
12 musicians, 18 actors,
8 writers, 6 visual artists,
6 dancers silenced in
21 countries

57
ATTACKS
57 cases of attacks on artists
or their artistic expression in
26 countries

48
IMPRISONED
31 musicians, 4 actors,
11 writers, 2 visual artists
silenced in 11 countries

88
PERSECUTED/THREATENED
37 musicians, 34 actors, 5 writers,
10 visual artists, 2 dancers silenced
in 35 countries

Source: Freemuse - *The State of Artistic Freedom 2018*

Literature
46 documented cases in 16 countries

Dance **12**
documented cases in 6 countries

Theatre
52
documented cases in 20 countries

**Art forms
SILENCED
in 2017**

Music **202** documented cases in 57 countries

Visual Arts
110
documented cases in 39 countries

Film **131**
documented cases in 36 countries

Source: Freemuse - *The State of Artistic Freedom 2018*

Censorship

An east-west shared value

73% of censorship cases committed by **government authorities**

A-List of blacklisting culture

China
55 ARTISTS
Mainly Hong Kong and Taiwanese musicians, filmmakers and actors. Banned by government blacklist

Uzbekistan
225 FILMS
Banned in one blacklist by government – mainly horror films – on indecency.

Malaysia
22 BOOKS
22 fictional and nonfictional books banned by the government for criticising the government and on the grounds of religion.

Turkey
31 ACTORS & ACTRESSES
Fired upon government closure of Diyarbakır Kurdish Theatre.

Ukraine
18 FILMS
Banned by government for being political and from conflicting countries.

Algeria
130 BOOKS
Banned by government, mainly for criticising the government and on the grounds of religion.

France
125 ARTWORKS
Censored by a court order on the grounds of indecency and misogyny.

UK
18 GANG MEMBERS
Prevented from making music videos and other expressions. Banned by court injunction on the grounds of hate speech and indecency.

Iran
10 FILMS
Banned by government for 'feminist and inappropriate themes'.

Top 10 Countries
found to have censored the most in 2017 (by number of art works and banned artists)

1.	Uzbekistan:	225
2.	France:	140
3.	Algeria:	132
4.	China:	67
5.	Turkey:	40
6.	USA:	31
7.	Malaysia:	26
8.	India & UK:	21
9.	Ukraine:	20
10.	Kenya:	16

Source: Freemuse – *The State of Artistic Freedom 2018*

This legitimising of the message of dismissing others' views in the West is well received by traditional repressive regimes in the global South and East who continue to clamp-down on civil society, journalists and artists, through taking over or weakening independent institutions. These neo-nationalist movements in the West, alongside old repressive regimes working together within weak international accountability frameworks, provide a governance structure for the new world culture of silencing others. This culture can be described with at least five common characteristics:

Firstly, violation of artistic freedom is a worldwide phenomenon. Violations of artistic freedom have gone beyond the stereotype of artists getting themselves in trouble for criticising governments in mostly repressive regimes in a handful of poor and less-developed countries. This report shows that 553 cases of violations took place in 78 countries, including in Europe and North America. Violations of minority rights to artistic freedom are found to have been practised almost equally (in number of violation incidents) in the Global North (48%) and Global South (52%). Six of the top ten censoring countries in 2017 are G20 member countries.

Secondly, the culture of silencing others is practiced by multiple actors. Violators are not only governments of repressive regimes. This research shows that they include governments from countries usually seen as open and democratic. Religious police and authorities actively restrict freedom of artistic expression in many countries. Non-state armed groups carried out attacks on civilians as they attempted to enjoy their cultural rights in the West and South. Many online and social media service companies violated artistic freedom by imposing arbitrary criteria for censoring artwork on their platforms, failing to observe international human rights standards to which they are also obliged. NGOs contribute to the culture of silencing others by calling for the censoring of artistic expression with which they disagree. Finally, professional associations representing artists' interests in many countries are powerful agents determining who can and cannot function within the cultural industries. They too can contribute to the culture of silencing others by, for example, penalising artists whose work contradicts their definition of indecency.

Thirdly, a new global culture of silencing others took place on communications and digital platforms. While censoring books, songs, films, theatre and visual arts was widely practised in 2017, violations of artistic freedom also took place on digital platforms. Many artists found that while their work was accessible to their audiences online, their commentary about their work or related issues through forums such as Twitter, Facebook, Instagram and others led them to be arrested and prosecuted. Internet censorship has become increasingly an effective tool to silence artists and people's expression of their views and creativity, while little progress has been made to bring accountability on governments' regulations on the use of internet and communication technologies.

Fourth, people play a more significant role in silencing others. This emerges in at least two forms. One is public support of populist-nationalist leaders in suppressing and silencing views considered non-mainstream, non-traditional or non-nationalistic. This is particularly the case in the US and Eastern European countries where such support has fuelled nationalism. The other role is through direct calls and pressure upon government and private entities for censorship, sometime accompanied by violent acts. In 2017, several cases were documented where such pressure was placed on museums and festivals to cancel or remove artwork on the ground of indecency, or seen to have insulted minority and LGBT groups.

Fifth, there is little accountability and justice for violations of artistic freedom. Unlike other human rights guaranteed in international human rights laws, violators of artistic freedom and related cultural rights have largely enjoyed impunity. From years of monitoring and documenting violations of artistic freedom, very few cases, if any, were known to have been brought to justice. Killers of artists tend to walk free. The same applies to those who persecute, threaten, attack, abduct and kidnap artists, not to mention prosecution and imprisonment carried out by the state.

Key to the impunity enjoyed by those who violate artistic freedom is the silencing of others through legislation. Many laws have been created and used to censor, raid, detain, prosecute and imprison artists, despite their failure to comply with international human rights treaties.

February 2018

www.freemuse.org

Key facts

- Freedom of speech is the right to seek, receive and impart information and ideas of all kinds, by any means. (page 1)

- Freedom of expression is a fundamental right protected under the Human Rights Act and under British common law. (page 2)

- 55 per cent of the 115 universities and students' unions we survey are this year ranked Red under our traffic-light rankings system, meaning they actively censor speech and ideas. (page 4)

- Over the past three years, students and/or student groups at 17 campuses have been punished for everything from criticising gay marriage on Facebook to organising a Thatcher vs the Miners themed party. (page 4)

- Google, which owns YouTube, launched a Pakistan-specific version, and introduced a process by which governments can request the blocking of access to offending material. (page 6)

- Roughly 36% of the world's population own a social media account. (page 11)

- The Ugandan government has introduced a 5% tax on social media usage. (page 11)

- The UK has one of the worst environments for press freedom in western Europe. (page 12)

- Italy was the only Western European country to have a lower ranking than the UK. (page 13)

- In the 2018 World Press Freedom Index, an annual report, by Reporters Without Borders (RSF), Britain was judged to have been in 40th place. (page 14)

- Iran was ranked at 164 on this year's press freedom list. (page 14)

- The United Arab Emirates is 128 on the World Ranking list. (page 15)

- Six years ago, just before Lord Leveson's inquiry into the 'culture and practices and ethics' of the British press, the UK was 12 places higher in the World Press Freedom Index. (page 16)

- At least 43 journalists have been killed in 2018. (page 17)

- 46 journalists were killed in 2017. (page 17)

- 2009 was the deadliest year for journalists, with 76 journalists killed worldwide. (page 17)

- A total of 74 were killed in 2012, making it the second deadliest year, while 73 were killed in 2015. (page 17)

- The most dangerous countries for journalists are Afghanistan, Syria, Mexico and Iraq. (page 17)

- At least 12 journalists have been killed so far in Afghanistan this year. (page 17)

- Mexico is the most dangerous for reporters because powerful drug cartels target journalists. (page 17)

- 47 journalists in Mexico have been killed since 1992. (page 17)

- Fake news is a tricky area for the law: it has not, generally, been illegal. (page 18)

- In France – 'fake news', necessarily narrowly defined so as to protect free speech, has been illegal since 1881. (page 18)

- Germany earlier this year also introduced an online hate speech law, giving platforms with more than two million users 24 hours to remove 'obviously illegal' terror content, racist material and fake news or face fines of up to €50 million (£44 million). (page 18)

- Malaysia has passed a law setting fines of up to £88,000 and jail terms of up to six years for offenders who use traditional news outlets, digital publications and social media – including outside Malaysia – to spread fake news. (page 18)

- While one in five children believe everything they read online is true, four in five do not. (page 21)

- More than half (54%) of 12- to 15-year-olds use social media platforms such as Facebook and Twitter, to access online news, making social media the second most popular source of news after television (62%). (page 22)

- Just 32% of 12- to 15-year-olds who say social media is one of their top news sources believe news accessed through these sites is always, or mostly, reported truthfully, compared to 59% who say this about TV and 59% about radio. (page 22)

- Four in ten teens (39%) say they have seen a fake news story online or on social media. (page 22)

- 63% of 12- to 15-year-olds who are aware of fake news are prepared to do something about it. (page 22)

- A recent survey of GoT viewer demographics found that 8.2% are under-18s. (page 28)

- Two-thirds of 11-to-15-year-olds use smartphones and most of them watch video online. (page 28)

- Teenagers consume one-third less broadcast TV on traditional sets than they did in 2010. (page 28)

- 26 per cent spike in suicide-related web searches after *13 Reasons Why* was released. (page 29)

- 93 per cent of viewers understand what the watershed is and 74 per cent think 9pm is the right time for it. (page 29)

- In Uzbekistan, 225 films were banned in one blacklist in 2017, while 130 books faced the same fate in Algeria. (page 36)

- On average, at least one artist was prosecuted per week in 2017. (page 36)

- Six of the top ten censoring countries in 2017 are G20 member countries. (page 39)

Censorship

When there are restrictions on what people can see or hear and on the information they are allowed to access, this is called censorship. By censoring something, an individual, publication or Government is preventing the whole truth from coming out or stopping something from being heard or seen at all. Items may also be censored or restricted to protect vulnerable people such as children, and to prevent public offence.

Classifications

Also called age ratings. Films in cinemas and on DVD, as well as computer games, must carry a classification indicating a minimum age at which the material should be watched or played. It is a criminal offence for a retailer to supply an age-restricted DVD or game to someone below the required age.

Defamation, libel and slander

The term 'defamation' refers to false claims made about an individual or group which present them in a negative and inaccurate light. When this takes a temporary form, for example in spoken comments, it is known as slander. When defamatory comments appear in a permanent form – i.e. they are communicated in writing or via a broadcast medium such as television – it is known as libel. Libel is a civil offence and should the person or group libelled wish to do so, they can pursue a claim against the originator of the defamatory comments through the courts.

Fake news

Fake news is false information; often spread by the internet, usually on social media, but sometimes by other media that appears to be true but is false. Sometimes it is done for financial or political gain.

Free press

A free press is one which is not censored or controlled by a government. It allows us to find out what we want to know without restrictions.

Freedom of expression

Also called freedom of speech, free speech. This is protected by Article 19 of the Universal Declaration of Human Rights, which states that: `Everyone has the right to freedom of opinion and expression; this right includes freedom to hold opinions without interference and to seek, receive and impart information and ideas through any media and regardless of frontiers`.

Gagging order

A ruling which prevents certain information from being made public. For example, if a court case is ongoing, the press can be prevented by law from publishing some of the

details if it is felt this would affect the outcome of the case – i.e. by influencing the jury and therefore preventing the defendant from having a fair trial.

Ofcom

The independent regulator for all radio, television and telecom broadcasting in the UK. Ofcom deal with all consumer complaints regarding television or radio, issue broadcasting licences and promote competition. Ofcom are Government-approved and act under the Communications Act 2003.

Press Complaints Commission

The PCC is a regulatory body responsible for ensuring that UK newspapers and magazines adhere to a Code of Practice. The Code aims to ensure responsible journalism by setting down rules on matters such as accuracy in reporting, privacy intrusion and media coverage of vulnerable groups. If a member of the public is affected by unfair media coverage, they can complain to the PCC, citing which part of the Code of Practice they feel has been breached. The Code was laid down by newspaper editors themselves, and the PCC consists of representatives of the major publishers: thus the newspaper industry is self-regulating.

The British Board of Film Classification (BBFC)

A body appointed by the government to classify all video and DVD releases.

The Freedom of Information Act

The Freedom of Information Act states that there should be free access to information about the Government, individuals and businesses.

The watershed

The watershed is the name for the 9pm cut-off point in television scheduling, after which television channels can show programmes containing material which may not have been suitable for a younger audience, such as scenes of a sexual nature or swearing.

Assignments

Brainstorming

⇨ In small groups, discuss what you know about censorship. Consider the following points:

- What is censorship?

- What is freedom of the press?

- What is free speech?

- Why are films and TV shows censored?

⇨ In pairs, create a list of pros and cons for censorship.

⇨ In small groups, create a mind-map of all the things, you think are, or could be, subject to censorship.

Research

⇨ Over the course of a week, look at news online (news sites, social media, etc.) and see how many stories you think could be 'fake news'. Write some notes on how to spot fake news.

⇨ Look at the map from the *World Press Freedom index 2018* and choose a country. Research censorship in that country and make some notes. See if you can find some case studies or examples of censorship in action.

⇨ Choose a book that has been banned and research why. Write some notes exploring why the book was banned and for what reasons. Feedback to your class.

Design

⇨ Design a poster that promotes freedom of expression.

⇨ Choose one of the articles in this book and create an illustration to highlight the key themes/message of your chosen article.

⇨ Using the article 'The state of artistic freedom', design a poster to promote freedom for artists.

⇨ Design a leaflet to help people spot fake news.

⇨ Using the article 'How deadly has 2018 been for journalists?', create an infografic about safety for journalists.

Oral

⇨ Talk to an adult you know about how DVD, film and television censorship has changed in their lifetime. Do they think that age-ratings have been relaxed? Is there more violence on TV? Ask them for some examples and then discuss your findings with your class.

⇨ Read the article 'The top ten things you need to know about freedom of expression laws' and create a five-minute presentation to teach 11- to 12-year-olds about the concept.

⇨ *'Freedom of speech is really important – but what if people want to say or write something really offensive? Should everyone be able to say exactly what they like?'.* Discuss this statement in pairs. Do you agree?

⇨ In small groups discuss the article 'What do protests about Harry Potter books teach us?' Do you think it is right for people to ban books? Do you agree that books can be damaging to children?

Reading/writing

⇨ Watch Iceland's banned Christmas advert. Write a letter to the advertising authority to either argue or support the banning of the advert.

⇨ Read Ray Bradbury's *Fahrenheit 451* and write a review exploring how the author deals with the theme of censorship.

⇨ Research the issue of censorship in Saudi Arabia. Write a one-page article for your school newspaper that explores the topic.

⇨ Write a one-paragraph definition of censorship.

⇨ Imagine the following situation: a child has been asked by their English teacher to read Harry Potter. Their parents feel very strongly that the book is inappropriate because of its themes of witchcraft, death and resurrection. Either:

- Write a letter from the point of view of the parent, explaining why you think the book should not be taught. Or,

- Write a letter from the point of view of the teacher, explaining why you think it would be inappropriate to prevent children from reading the book.

⇨ In pairs or small groups write a 500-word fake news story which could fool your classmates. Create some fake research or data that may persuade people that your story is real. Include things which could make your story seem more reliable.

Acknowledgements

The publisher is grateful for permission to reproduce the material in this book. While every care has been taken to trace and acknowledge copyright, the publisher tenders its apology for any accidental infringement or where copyright has proved untraceable. The publisher would be pleased to come to a suitable arrangement in any such case with the rightful owner.

Images

All images courtesy of iStock except pages 7, 16, 19, 31, 38: Pixabay and 2, 4, 11, 13, 17, 18, 26, 27, 29, 33, 34, 35, 39: Unsplash

Icons

Icons on pages 8, 13, 22, 23, 38 were made by Freepik from www.flaticon.com.

Illustrations

Don Hatcher: pages 3 & 6. Simon Kneebone: pages 10 & 15. Angelo Madrid: pages 11 & 36.

Additional acknowledgements

With thanks to the Independence team: Shelley Baldry, Tina Brand, Danielle Lobban, Jackie Staines and Jan Sunderland.

Tracy Biram

Cambridge, January 2019